MW00453200

Praise for Author Doug Eastwood

A thoroughly researched and compelling story of one family's tragedy and its lasting impact. Doug Eastwood brings the Malloy family to life and draws us into their story.

Jody Dudycha

Pretty much everything that happens in, and around, Las Vegas can eventually lead to a story. The fact this story actually happened will make people want to read this book. I started reading and it immediately held my interest. I could not put it down until I read the last page. I felt like I knew the characters and felt empathy for their plight. It is a very good read. I hope Doug writes more stories in the near future.

Fred Fricke

In an era when Americans routinely stopped to help each other, a killer uses their goodwill to lure caring people into his grasp. The unthinkable happens, and the public shudders. A true story that keeps you riveted as a family, community and country learn the truth about the shocking events of that day. A well-written book.

Gary Mauri

One great read with plenty of cliff hangers. I can see a movie in the making.
John Brunning

Ultimately this is a story of redemption.

Mike Blackburn

I was captivated from the first paragraph. It became a must read when I realized it was based on an actual old case file. There is nothing more interesting than reality.

Jeff Crowe

Certainly inspires a person to know the story. Mystery, relationships and a lot of unknown.

Sandi Bloem

A real spellbinder.

Dean Haagenson

Closure Can Be a Myth

The True Story of a Family Tragedy
in the Las Vegas Desert

DOUG EASTWOOD

Closure Can be a Myth
The True Story of a Family Tragedy in the Las Vegas Desert

Copyright © Doug Eastwood

All rights reserved. No part of this book may be reproduced, scanned, or distributed in any print, electric or audio form, without written permission by the author.

Based on a true crime, this tragic story unfolds in early 1964. A horrific crime leaving an aftermath of devastation. Some of the victim's loved ones were able to find healing and move on from the tragedy that so effectively disrupted their lives. Others were not so lucky and could find no comfort, peace or closure from the emptiness left by the unimaginable horrors that took place in the Nevada desert.

Names of the characters in the book have been changed, except for the victims, the victim's family members, and the accused. The majority of the information contained within the book came from public sources and family members.

Published By: Bitterroot Mountain Publishing House

Edited by Suzanne Holland, M. S.

ISBNs:
978-1-960059-13-0 (softcover)
1-978-960059-14-7 (hardcover)
978-1-960059-12-3 (ebook)

Library of Congress Cataloging in Publication Data

PRINTED IN THE UNITED STATES OF AMERICA

First Edition

Contents

PART ONE

CHAPTER ONE

Unusually Late

N orma Widick returned home from work Friday afternoon. She breezed through the doorway, and headed straight into the bedroom to change out of her office clothes into something more comfortable. She thought about where she and her husband might go for dinner that evening. A new Mexican restaurant just opened in nearby Baldwin Park named the El Hacienda. That would be her recommended destination for their dinner date.

Gaynard usually arrived home about 20 to 30 minutes after Norma each day. She knew it would be at least an hour before they would enter the restaurant, so she went into the kitchen to grab a snack. She took an apple out of the fruit bowl and a paring knife from the drawer. Standing at the counter, something caught her attention in her peripheral vision. The back door looked slightly ajar. Thinking that Gaynard might be home and parked his truck out back, she went to the door calling to him before she opened it. "Sweetheart are you home?" There came no answer as she reached for the door knob and pulled the door open.

At first, she did not recognize what she saw on the concrete walkway. Then she saw pennies strewn amongst shards of glass that glittered in the afternoon sunlight. *What is this?* There were hundreds of pennies mixed in among the broken glass. She felt angry, and then panic crept into her mind. The back door slightly ajar, broken glass, and pennies. "We've been robbed!" she said out loud.

She turned, racing toward the phone to call the police. Panic and fear overcame her as she realized that someone might still be in the house. Then she saw it, and froze. Her eyes widened, shock replaced fear and panic. She felt like her heart skipped a beat. Norma's hand went to her chest. A feeling of defeat and loss came over her when she noticed the missing object.

"Oh no, please no," she said aloud. Her heart still racing, she took a cursory look around the room; nothing else seemed to be out of place. She nervously walked through the house; no drawers were pulled out, nothing else seemed disturbed. The rest of the house seemed to be undisturbed.

She realized that the broken glass on the walkway could only be their coin bottle. Norma and Gaynard put all their loose change in a five-gallon glass Sparklett's bottle for over a year. Now, it's missing from their living room. The change included pennies, nickels, dimes, quarters, fifty cent pieces and an occasional one or five-dollar bill. Her heart sank as she thought about the fifty cent pieces. Those coins were recently minted and carried the profile of John F. Kennedy, the nation's beloved president, assassinated just four months earlier.

Norma went to the phone and dialed the Alhambra Police station to report the burglary.

Waiting for the police to arrive, she reflected on seeing Gaynard off to work earlier that morning. She envisioned him picking up the keys to his truck, tossing them back and forth between his hands a few times as he headed to the front door on his way to work. He said to me, "Hey, Mrs. Widick, where are you taking me for dinner tonight?" I walked over to where he stood, laced my fingers behind the upper button on his shirt and pulled him to me. I gave him a kiss and said, "I think I will surprise you." He smiled, gave me a big hug, turned, and walked out the door. I watched him walk toward his pick-up truck. As he stepped into the vehicle, he winked at me and said, "I love you. See you tonight." He'll be so disappointed when he gets home and learns that we have been robbed.

Gaynard and Norma Widick exchanged marital vows seven months earlier. They dated for the better part of a year before exchanging vows. He was five years older than Norma. She just turned twenty-two. Gaynard, an acquaintance of her older brother, Mitchell, they attended the same high school in San Gabriel, California.

A chance encounter brought them together one day when Gaynard dialed up her parents' house hoping to reconnect with Mitchell. Norma, who stopped by to visit her parents, answered the phone. The two of them talked for a while, catching up on what they have been doing since high school. Gaynard asked her if she would like to join him and some friends that were going to the horse races on Saturday at the Santa Anita Park. Nestled up against the San Gabriel Mountains, the race track and its surroundings were picturesque. Norma accepted the invitation. Soon, the two of them became inseparable.

Photo source: Doug Eastwood
Santa Anita Park

Two police officers arrived fifteen minutes after she notified the P.D. of a possible theft. The officer who came to the door introduced himself as Officer Hughes. He asked her, "Is there anyone else in the house?" She told him she did not think so. The other officer walked around to the rear of the house. The police did a room by room sweep, just to be safe. They also took a look in the detached garage behind the house. They asked Norma to lead them through her discovery of the broken bottle, including the time she arrived home that afternoon.

Norma said, "My husband and I have been putting our change into a Sparklett's bottle for almost a year and a half. We started doing that before we got married. We were doing it on a whim. A friend gave me an empty 5-gallon bottle and thought it would be interesting to see how long it took to fill it up. It became a habit where we would drop our spare change and a few special coins into the jar and grew a savings that we would eventually count up and use it to do something fun. The bottle became a conversation piece amongst friends and relatives as it began to fill up with coins and a few small bills. Everyone tried to guess how much money the big jar could hold."

"Is that all that is missing?" asked Hughes.

"I think so. I became terrified when I first discovered the back door open and the broken bottle on the walkway. I looked around hastily and did not see anything else that seemed out of place."

The officers walked around the outside of the house and noted that none of the windows were open, and no indication of anyone tampering with the locks on the doors. There were no signs of forced entry, no broken windows.

Hughes asked, "What are the chances that you, or your husband, did not lock the back door when you left for work this morning? Perhaps the front door did not get locked when you left for work this morning and the entry occurred through that door. The person that did this let themselves out the back door. Someone knew about the coin jar, and wanted it for themselves, or just the contents, since the remnants of the jar are scattered on the walkway."

Norma thought about that for a moment. "I would have been the last one out this morning. It is pretty habitual for me to lock the doors on my way out. I check the back door to make sure it is locked and I leave by the front door. I don't think I left them open, but I suppose it is possible."

"Mrs. Widick," said Officer Hughes, "This does not appear to be a random burglary. I think someone specifically targeted your spare change bottle, someone who knows about it, and someone you probably know. I would bet that bottle to be pretty heavy considering all the coins making it awkward to carry. Look closely at the carpet in the living room, there are tell-tale signs that the bottle could have been dragged to the back door. The thief might have tried to roll it out the back door, but it hit too hard on the concrete walkway when it rolled off the threshold. That's where it shattered. Whoever did this, did not seem to be in a big hurry. The thief took more than a little bit of time to gather up the coins. What do you estimate the dollar amount of the money to be in the jar?" asked Hughes.

"The best guess is that it could be upwards of $2,000 when it is full. We were pretty close to seeing the change reach the top of the bottle."

"That's a lot of money to have out in the open for everyone to see," said Hughes.

"I suppose we viewed it as another piece of the furniture. It's probably one of the few things that appreciates in value the more we use it." She said in a light but nervous laugh. "It's always been in the living room area."

"We would like to talk to your husband." A crime like this is hard to solve, especially if it involves someone you know. We will talk to your neighbors to see if any of them noticed anything peculiar during the day. What time does your husband get home?"

Norma glanced at the clock; 6:00 p.m. "My husband should have been home by now. We were planning to go to dinner tonight. Can I have him call you when he gets here?"

"Yes," the officer handed her a card. "He can contact us at this number. We would like to know if there is anyone either of you might suspect that could have done this. As I mentioned earlier, this does not appear to be a break and entry type of burglary; someone deliberately came for your large bank bottle."

The officers talked to a few of Norma's neighbors, wrapped up their work and left the residence.

Norma felt exhausted. She did not have an appetite to go out for dinner. The heart pounding moment when she thought about being burglarized, coupled by the police thinking that someone they knew stole their savings jar, caused her to just want to retreat into her home, and into the arms of her husband.

Photo source: Doug Eastwood
A 5-gallon glass Sparkletts bottle 19" tall

She phoned Gaynard's parents to see if by chance he stopped by their house on his way home from work. He did not stop there, and they have not heard from him. Norma told them about all the excitement when she got home from work a few hours ago, including the police believing that the theft could have been by someone they knew.

Her mother-in-law expressed how disappointed Gaynard will be when he finds out. She said, "The two of you were so diligent putting the change in the bottle for so long. Is there anything you need? Anything I can do for you?"

"No, thank you. I will talk to you later, after Gaynard comes home."

Next, she contacted Gaynard's work place. She thought maybe he worked late and didn't get the opportunity to call home to let her know. Gaynard worked at the Firestone Tire Distribution Center in Los Angeles, about 10 miles from their rental home. Firestone Tire supplied the Ford Motor Company with nearly all their tire needs since the early 1900's. That exclusive partnership, and other tire distributors purchases, saw Firestone become very busy. The L.A. site recently started running two shifts, six days a week. Gaynard worked the day shift, which ended at 4:30 p.m. However, overtime work became more frequent, and she assumed that could be what kept him from coming home on time this afternoon.

An office worker answered the phone. Norma explained why she contacted them. Disappointed, and a bit puzzled, she learned that no one from the day shift worked overtime that afternoon or early evening. She thought, he's not working overtime, and he has not stopped by his parents' house. Where is he? Wherever he stopped at on his way home from work, he should have been able to reach me.

Norma sat down on the couch and wondered if she missed something. The conversation she and the officer had played over and over in her mind. She thought hard about the officer suggestion that she might have left one of the doors unlocked. I'm sure I locked the doors when I left this morning, I'm certain of it. No other items were missing from the house. Did I miss something regarding my husband? Could Gaynard have broken the bottle and taken the money? He recently withdrew some funds from our joint account. He told me he loaned the money to a friend at work. The loan has not yet been paid back, and re-deposited in our account. Her feelings were experiencing a mixture of anger and sadness. The money in the jar could have been used for a fun vacation; a second honeymoon. Perhaps they could have used the money for a down payment on a house of their own.

She reflected on Gaynard's demeanor. He seemed upbeat and happy when he left for work this morning. We made plans to go out tonight. He did not engage in conversations like he used to. She thought it might be due to stress at work. Now she wished she would have pressed the issue a bit more. Excusing her concerns as simply being over-worried, she glanced at the clock. Norma realized Gaynard should have been home three hours ago. He has never been this late getting home from work. She thought about calling mutual friends, but decided to wait. He might walk through the door any minute.

Norma turned on the TV to help pass the time. The clock now read just past 8:00 p.m., and the local broadcasting companies did not offer a lot to watch. The house seemed empty to her, quiet and lonely. The TV, if for nothing else, provided background noise.

She began to wonder if her brother, Mitchell, could give her any insight into what Gaynard could be doing. *Should I try to reach him?* she thought to herself. No, our relationship has been strained for the past several years. Besides, Mitchell has isolated himself, and always seems to be angry. I could call my cousin, Sandy Marion. We celebrated all our milestones together: high school graduation, our first jobs, turning twenty-one, getting engaged.

She shook her head, confirming she would wait until tomorrow before calling her friends. Now, more than ever, she and Gaynard needed to talk privately. She stood up, turned the TV off and walked into the bedroom to try and get some sleep.

Photo source: Sandy Marion
Cousins Sandy and Norma
Celebrating Norma's 21ˢᵗ Birthday in Palm Springs.

CHAPTER TWO

Uneasy Feeling

The morning sunshine peaked through the window as Norma awoke from a restless sleep. She glanced at the clock on the night stand, it read 6:10 a.m. Hurriedly swinging her feet off the bed, throwing on a robe, she walked into the living room hoping Gaynard returned home. He wasn't there. Norma could not shake the uneasy feeling that something very wrong happened to him. Looking into the backyard, she hoped Gaynard parked his truck near the garage. No truck, he did not make it home all night. She looked out the front door, no truck in front of the house, or in the driveway. Panic began creeping back into her thoughts, replacing worry, as Norma wondered what could have happened to him.

Thinking the worst, she dialed the phone number on the card the officers gave her yesterday. Norma's hands were shaking, and she found it difficult to dial the phone. Her heart began pounding faster when the police operator answered. She stumbled through her explanation for the call. The operator told her to hold for a moment and transferred her to Sergeant Roseborough in the patrol division. She told the Sergeant everything that occurred since yesterday afternoon and that her husband did not return home Friday night after work. She emphasized he has never done anything like this and that he would always call her if he would be late getting home. Missing all night, no word from him could only mean that something is wrong, and he needs help. Norma felt a tear roll down her cheek. Both eyes began to tear, and her voice began to crack as she spoke to the sergeant.

"Mrs. Widick," said the sergeant, "I know this is difficult for you. I need to get some information so we can start a more thorough search for your husband. I have in front of me the report from yesterday's burglary/robbery investigation at your home. Can you give me a description of Gaynard: age, height, weight, color of hair, color of eyes, any distinguishing factors that will help us?"

Norma, wiping tears from her eyes, struggling to stay calm, her nose sniffling, she began to give a detailed description of her husband. She told the sergeant that Gaynard stood about 5 feet, 8 inches in height. He weighed approximately 150 pounds, dark brown hair and brown eyes, no facial hair. She felt overwhelmed by her emotions and began to cry audibly into the phone.

"I'm sorry," she blurted, "I'm so worried. I can't stop crying."

The sergeant waited a moment and said, "I know this is difficult for you. Can you describe the vehicle he drives; make, model, color, year, and license plate number." Norma took several deep breaths then told the sergeant that Gaynard drove a light brown 1955 Ford pick-up. License plate number is MHD 923. She noticed her hands continued to shake and tears streamed down her cheeks as she held the phone.

He told her they would send out a notice to the patrol officers in the Alhambra PD, and to surrounding police jurisdictions, including Los Angeles.

The sergeant said, "Currently, we do not have any reports of a vehicle accident involving the description of your husband's pick-up truck. Neither do we have reports from all the other jurisdictions, so I will follow that up and get back to you. Give me a number where I can reach you when I have more information."

"Do you think he could have been in an accident and is in the hospital?" she asked.

"I am doubtful of that," said the sergeant. "You would have been the first to be notified if your husband were in an accident, regardless of where it may have occurred. Is there any chance that you fell asleep and did not hear the phone ring?"

"I don't think so. I don't think I got any sleep worrying about him."

"All right, the responding officers made a note that states your husband works at the Firestone Tire Center in L.A. Is that correct?" asked the sergeant.

"Yes," Norma said.

The sergeant read another note on the officer's report to himself. They spoke to a Mrs. Saunders, who lives directly across the street. She stated that she is pretty sure she saw Gaynard's truck in the driveway shortly after noon, maybe 12:30 p.m. She could not be 100% sure that it was Gaynard's truck. She did not know the make or model of the vehicle, but it had been a brown pick-up truck, the same color as Gaynard's. She did not see the vehicle leave the residence.

The sergeant said, "There are only two, maybe three, possible hospital locations that he could have been transported to within the corridor between his work, and your home. We will contact the hospitals to see if anyone admitted matches Gaynard Widick's description. I suggest you begin calling mutual friends to find out if they know of his whereabouts," said the sergeant. "I will contact you later this morning, or early this afternoon. Is there anything else I can do for you?"

"Thank you for your help, I'll start contacting our friends," and she hung up.

Norma immediately called her closest friend, her older sister, Margie. Ten years older than Norma, Margie married a man named Jimmy Mauri. They soon became a family of five by adding three kids: Gary (8-years-old), Beth Ann (6-years-old), and Lisa the youngest (at 2-years-old).

Gary answered the phone, surprised and happy to be talking to his Aunt Norma on Saturday morning.

"Are you coming over?" he asked excitedly. "I can't wait to see you."

Norma felt a sense of calm by just hearing her nephew's voice.

"There is nothing I'd rather do than spend time around you and your sisters today," she said. "What are your plans for the day?"

"Dad said he will take us to the park a little later. He wants to watch us burn up some energy on the jungle gym."

Norma laughed, she knew the kids were an endless store of energy, and she loved being around them. Then she said, "Gary, I am sorry, but I don't think I can come over to visit today. But I will be there as soon as I can get away. I do need to talk to your mom. Is she there and can you put her on the phone? Thank you, I love you."

"I love you, Aunt Norma, I'll get my mom for you."

Margie, shocked, almost to the point of being speechless, about hearing the details of events that occurred since yesterday afternoon. Norma told her sister the police asked her to contact their mutual friends, and she wanted Margie to help her do that. The two sisters made a list of people to contact. They agreed to keep the information they shared amongst their friends to a minimum. They knew that no matter what they said, some people were going to be alarmed.

Margie said, "We should let our friends know that Gaynard did not return home from work Friday night, and that the police have been contacted. Also, that you are deeply worried."

"Thanks for your help, Margie. I appreciate this. I'll call the folks first and let them know what has happened," said Norma.

Margie told her husband, Jimmy, about her conversation with Norma. Jimmy looked as shocked as Margie felt. He knew that his sister-in-law must be beside herself worrying about her husband.

"I'm going to contact some of our friends, and then I'll probably go see Norma," she said.

Norma listened as the phone rang at her parents' house. Her mother answered.

"Mom, something's wrong," her voice started to crack, "I don't know what to do."

"Talk to me, how can I help?" her mom said.

Norma took a moment to compose herself, "Gaynard did not come home last night. I stayed up most of the night, hoping, expecting him to walk in and now I am starting to panic. When I got home from work yesterday, I thought we'd been burglarized. I found our coin bottle broken into pieces in the back yard. All the money we saved in the bottle for the past year or more is gone.

"Yesterday, I called the police to report the burglary. I notified them this morning to tell them Gaynard did not return home. They're checking accident reports, and suggested I contact our mutual friends to see if anyone knows something about where Gaynard might be. Margie's helping me get in touch with our friends. I've no idea what could have happened to him. I'm so worried. What should I do?" She broke down sobbing as she spoke to her mother.

"Norma," Inez said, "I know how you must feel. Let's take this one step at a time. It's good the police are involved in case something has happened and he needs help. Contact your friends, someone might know something. I will talk to your dad and see if he might have any ideas on what we can do. I will get back to you soon. Start reaching out to your friends, sweetheart."

Next, Norma talked to John Hindson, one of Gaynard's co-workers. The two men knew each other for a couple of years, before Norma and Gaynard became engaged. She knew John and his wife, Diane, from social events she and Gaynard attended. The four of them went out together for dinner on several occasions. *I like them, they have become good friends to Gaynard and me. I hate making these phone calls.* After only a few rings, John answered the phone.

After a brief exchange of greeting one another, Norma said, "John, I am trying to locate Gaynard. He did not come home last night. Do you know where I can find him?"

"Oh no," he replied. "He left work early yesterday, saying something about an emergency. Has something happened to him? Is there something I can do to help you?"

"He left work *early?*" she asked. "I'm trying to find out where he might be. Do you know if he left work early any other times?"

"I don't know that, but I suppose I can ask personnel about his time sheets without creating any suspicion. Let's see what I can do, and I'll get back to you," said John.

"I'm sorry to have bothered you. Thank you, we'll talk later." She gently put down the phone. *He left work early because of an emergency?* John is probably wondering what is going on, since I didn't know what Gaynard could be doing, and he did not come home.

John Hindson recently accepted a supervisory position at the Firestone distribution center. That led to more hours as the center started operating six days a week. Gaynard did not seem interested in taking on a new role at work. He seemed quite satisfied working in shipping and receiving. He understood that part of the job, and he did it quite well. She felt comfortable talking to Gaynard's co-worker, but now she felt a little embarrassed that she knew nothing of her husband's whereabouts.

Spending the next couple of hours talking to friends, she heard the same response from each of them; no one has heard, or seen Gaynard in the past 24 to 48 hours.

Then she heard a knock on the front door. Moving quickly toward the door, her heart racing, she knew it would be Gaynard.

The door opened before she could get to it. Her sister Margie walked in.

"I drove over from Glendora to keep you company and help sort things out. I tried calling to let you know I would be coming over. But the line rang busy, so I thought you were probably still talking to people, and I decided to just get in the car and drive here."

The two sisters were close friends, even though they were 10 years apart in age. Norma knew she could always confide in her older sister, and she trusted her implicitly.

Margie, appearing baffled, said that she contacted everyone on her list and no one has heard from him since last week.

"I know how frustrating this must be for you. Is there any possibility that he took another route home, maybe a scenic route through the foothills? Maybe the truck went off the road and is in a canyon."

"I suppose anything is possible. I just learned that he left work early yesterday. He could have driven a different route home. The San Gabriel Mountains would be somewhat out of the way. That's what worries me. It does not make any sense that he would not come home or try to call if he were not in some kind of trouble," said Norma.

"Maybe he fell and bumped his head. He could be experiencing a loss of memory—amnesia. He might not know where he is or how to get home. Maybe someone robbed him, hit in the head and he's unconscious."

"Margie," said Norma. "This is *not* helping. You're making me worry *more*."

"Norma, I apologize, we all want to know where he could be. I am going to be blunt and ask you. Do you think there could be another woman involved?"

Shocked by the question, Norma took several moments before she could respond. "I honestly do not think there is, or I don't want to believe that's a possibility. I want to believe he loves me and is dedicated to our marriage. He knows I love him. I'm just not so sure about everything.

"I don't understand the discrepancies in our savings account. He apparently took money out to loan to a friend at his work place, but it's never been paid back. He has been acting more withdrawn lately. I don't know what would keep him out all night, but I'm certain it is not another woman. He did not take any extra clothes. Besides the money in the jar, there is nothing else missing from the house."

Margie looked at her younger sister. "I can see your pain and uncertainty. I wish I could make it all go away. But I can't. I'm afraid that the best I can do is to be here for you. We'll take this moment by moment, day by day, if necessary, until we find some answers."

Then Norma's phone rang. Gaynard's mother wanted to know if he made it home.

Norma sighed. "No, I still don't know what is going on. I just learned that he apparently left work early yesterday for some kind of an emergency. I've spoken to a lot of our friends and no one has heard from him. Earlier this morning, I contacted the police to find out if they knew of any reports of an accident matching his vehicle description. No accident, no contact, nothing to report."

His mother reiterated how uncharacteristic this is for Gaynard not to come home, or call. Norma could tell that her mother-in-law is also deeply worried. Norma said she would let her know if she learned anything new, and asked Karen to call her if she heard from him. She assured Norma that she would.

"Norma," Margie said, "how about if you come to our house tonight for dinner, and we can talk some more?"

"That sounds like a good idea, being around the kids will help take my mind off of the uncertainty. But I should probably stay here in case Gaynard comes home or the police call this number if they need to contact me."

"Well, all right. I'd rather have you stay at our house, but I understand your wanting to be at home. I am going to call you first thing in the morning. If anything happens before then, or if you need to talk, you know how to reach me," said Margie. They gave each other a big hug and Margie left for home.

Norma tried to busy herself around the house to pass the time, but her worry kept bringing her back to what might have possibly happened to her husband. She went for a walk, hoping that would relax her, and help her think straight. Then she worried that the phone would ring, and she would not be there to answer it in her short absence. She walked into the house around 4:00 P.M. and heard the phone ringing.

The voice on the other end of the phone said, "This is Sergeant Roseborough from the Alhambra PD, we spoke earlier today about your husband not returning home."

"Yes," Norma said and blurted out, "has Gaynard been in an accident? Have you located him?"

"No, to both of your questions," he said. "I am calling to let you know, we have contacted other outlying police departments and the hospitals. So far, there are no reports of an accident. I wanted you to know that we sent out a bulletin county wide that included the description of the truck and your husband.

"If one of our patrolmen spots the vehicle, he will stop it. However, we can only let your husband know that you have been trying to find him. We cannot make him go home. That is his choice. Mrs. Widick, I know this is a sensitive subject for you, but I have to ask. Is your relationship with your husband strained at this time? Is there a reason he would leave and not want to go home? My reason for asking is that quite often when someone disappears, like your husband has, they don't want to be found. More often than not, it is the result of a stressed, or disintegrating relationship."

Surprised by what the sergeant just told her, she began to protest a bit to the officer. "Our relationship is healthy and good. We made plans for dinner last night. I cannot find a reasonable answer as to why he would not come home. He didn't take anything with him: no clothes, no toiletry items, nothing that would sustain time away from home. I wouldn't have called you if I were not worried about him. I feel like I'm going crazy from all this worry. He has no history of ever doing something like this. I've talked to all of our friends, and no one has heard from him." Norma's voice began to crack as tears rolled down her cheeks.

"Mrs. Widick," he said, "I did not mean to upset you. I need for you to understand that we will keep an eye out for your husband, but we cannot bring him home to you. He is an adult, and has the right to leave and stay away if he wants."

Norma felt awful. Things seem to be going from bad to worse. Something is wrong, she thought, very wrong! He's in trouble, and I know it!

The rest of the day went by painfully slow. That evening she made herself a peanut butter and jelly sandwich, poured herself a glass of milk and sat down on the couch.

She started thinking about the plans that she made, the plans that she and Gaynard made before they were married.

Norma set her sights on a law degree. She attended evening classes at the local community college in order to get some of the preliminary classes out of the way. A typical two-year program at a community college, is free to California residents, other than purchasing an ASB card and small health services fee. She also held a job at a title insurance company. She contacted the University of California at Los Angeles (UCLA) regarding their law program. She planned to attend UCLA after completing her two-year degree. Full tuition is required to attend the university. Her parents said they would like to help her pay for the tuition. She hesitated on entering UCLA right away as that would require her to quit working and focus all of her attention on a law degree. Delaying the process would allow her to buy a car, and save some money; both of which she deemed necessary.

When she and Gaynard decided to marry, they discussed their future plans: Norma's education, buying a home, and raising a family. Norma put a temporary hold on her pursuit of a law degree, so the two of them could concentrate on their marriage, and all the benefits of two people sharing their lives together. Putting her plans on hold would be worth the wait.

Gaynard, on the other hand, did not talk much to her about his future at Firestone Tire, or what he might want to do in the next five to ten years. The work he did at Firestone felt rewarding, the pay was good, and he developed friendly relationships with quite a few of his co-workers.

Her thoughts drifted back to her childhood, to the small mid-western town of Fort Dodge, Iowa. She reflected on the fun times growing up in the mid-west. The summers were hot and sometimes it could get quite humid. She learned to swim in one of the nearby lakes. On occasion her family would travel to the nearby Missouri River. That river seemed so big to her as a child until she saw the vastness of the Pacific Ocean.

The winters in Iowa could be very cold. Sometimes there would be a lot of snow. People adjust to the conditions, and kids are the most adaptable to the environment. Sledding, building snow men, and the inevitable snow-ball fights were winter highlights.

Her family moved to San Gabriel, California when Norma turned nine years old. Saying good-bye to her friends seemed like it would always be a sad day in her life. However, she adapted quickly to her new home in Southern California. Warm weather almost all the time and she made lots of new friends.

Norma recalled that her sister Margie, did not embrace the same excitement about the move. Margie finished high school a year earlier, so it was more difficult for her to leave her friends. Mitchell, her older brother, just entered his sophomore year of high school when they left Iowa. He seemed angry when they moved, and that anger seemed to steadily increase. She never understood why he seemed to be so unhappy. Never the less, she gave him room and did not criticize him, or attempt to correct his attitude, or give him advice. In return, her older brother never paid much, if any, attention to her.

She thought about her own high school days. High school could not have been more fun. I was cute with a bubbly, outgoing, and friendly personality. I felt popular among my classmates. Track and field became my choice of sports. I participated in those events all four years. The team relay, 200 meter and 400-meter race were the events I excelled in. Running came easy; maybe my lighter frame allowed me to run so effortlessly. I enjoyed the team camaraderie; a big part of the high school social scene.

She laughed out loud thinking about her attempt to participate in the hurdles. Her first attempt could be described as a bit of a disaster. Her front leg did not get quite high enough to clear the hurdle. Her legs and the hurdle tangled as she fell hard on the ground, face first. She cut the lower side of her right jaw when she fell on the dirt track. The cut cleared up nicely over time, but she always thought that it left a small scar, something no one saw until she pointed it out.

She liked to run long distances, pacing herself for upwards of 3 to 5 miles. Running became a hobby and a passion. She often expressed her disappointment that cross country running, for girls, did not rise up as a recognized sport in high school. When she introduced Gaynard to running, he did not like it. 'Leave the running to those who want to run. It's not for me,' he would often tell her.

Life is good, I met someone that I admire, and love very much. Our time together has been wonderful. So, what is going on now? Why do I suddenly feel so afraid and insecure?

She looked at the TV screen, her eyes opened wide, realizing she must have dozed briefly. George Putnam sat behind his desk broadcasting on the screen, which meant it must be around 10:00 p.m. He became a well-known news anchor that broadcasted every week day at 5:00 p.m. and 10:00 p.m. He coined a catchy phrase that he used at the end of every broadcast. George would end the news by saying, "And that's the up-to-the-minute news, up-to-the-minute, that's all the news." He concluded the 5:00 p.m. broadcast by adding to this phrase; 'Back at 10, see you then." Everyone in the Southland recognized George Putnam. Relaxing back on the couch, Norma drifted into a restless sleep.

Glancing at the clock, it read 2:30 a.m. Norma rose from the couch. She peered out the back door and then the front door, but did not see Gaynard's truck in the yard. Worry and confusion dominated her thoughts.

"Where are you?" her worried voice carried through the house. "Have you been in an accident? Are you hurt? Were you robbed? Are you injured and can't call me?"

CHAPTER THREE

Vanished

Norma's nights became increasingly restless and sleepless. The events of the past two days wore her down. Her worries turned to fear that something terrible happened to her husband. Where is he? She wondered why no one knew of his whereabouts since Friday, two days ago.

Around noon she heard a knock on the front door. Carrying groceries, Inez and Margie entered the house. They both looked like they too struggled to get a good night's sleep, worrying about Gaynard and Norma.

"I thought you could use some more company and tagged along with your sister. Dad is going to try and stop by later this afternoon. Your Uncle Chuck is at the house. He and Dad are replacing the kitchen faucets. I told Chuck about Gaynard's disappearance. How are you doing, sweetheart?"

Norma hugged them both and replied, "I'm doing as well as can be expected. Although I'm not getting much sleep."

Inez went in the kitchen to make some coffee. The three of them sat around the kitchen table and began talking about what could have happened to Norma's missing husband.

"I brought Mom up to speed," said Margie, "regarding your contacting the police department, and both of us calling everyone we can think of. And yet, we still have no idea what might have happened to Gaynard."

Inez said, "I doubt that he has been in an accident. The police would have heard something by now. It's been more than 48 hours, and they

21

would have contacted you if something happened to him. The fact that no one has heard from him is very puzzling. If he did come home early on Friday, broke the savings jar, as you suspect, he would have enough money to sustain himself for a while. I cannot imagine him doing that. Observing the two of you add your change to that jar for over a year always created an anticipation of the moment it would fill up. How much money do you think that big bottle could hold?"

Norma thought, it's so much more than just the money. We imagined a special trip together. What we might have done, or could have done, with the money would create good memories of our journey together. Now it's all gone.

"I told the police that Gaynard and I guessed it could hold nearly $2,000," said Norma.

Inez and her daughters explored multiple possibilities of what might have happened to Gaynard, eventually discounting all of them.

Inez asked, "Norma, is there the remotest possibility that he ran off with someone? I would not ask you that, but why would he break your spare change bank, take the money and nothing else? There would have been enough money from that jar to sustain him for a while."

Margie fidgeted in her chair, "I asked Norma the same question yesterday."

Norma thought, if I keep getting asked this, I might start to believe it is possible. How well can you really know someone? Was a year of dating too short? We have only been married seven months. Stay calm. Norma looked back and forth between her mother and sister.

"I really don't think so. As bad and hurtful as that might be, I don't think there is even a remote chance of that. Maybe I'm being naïve, but I just can't see him doing that."

Margie, seeing the pain in her sister's eyes said, "I tend to agree. It would be hard to hide a clandestine relationship from everyone. No one that we talked to, including his parents, have any idea where he has gone. Nothing adds up, especially since no one has heard from him, or seen him. When you spoke to his work place, did they give you any idea what the emergency could be that caused him to leave work early on Friday?"

Before Norma could answer, the phone rang. Karen wanted to find out if Norma heard anything new regarding Gaynard.

"Margie and my mom are here. We believe that he probably has not been in an accident. I would have heard from the police by now. It's maddening not to know anything. You will be the first person I call when I do hear something."

"I appreciate that," Karen said. "Norma, this is very confusing. Floyd and I were talking last night. Let me ask you a question, did you and Gaynard buy a new car recently, or were you considering buying one?"

Norma thought that to be an odd question. They both brought vehicles into the marriage: his truck, her car. They liked what they were driving, and she could not think of any reason why either one of them would be considering another vehicle at this time.

"No, we didn't buy a new car, and we haven't been talking about it either. Why do you ask?"

"Norma, we don't have any idea what is going on, or what might have happened to him. Floyd and I talked about your Sparkletts bottle being broken and the money taken. We wondered, if Gaynard could have possibly taken the money. Our concern grew, and that's why I wanted to ask about the car purchase. A few weeks ago, he borrowed $500.00 from Floyd and me. He said the two of you were buying a new car, and he needed it for a down payment. He found a car he wanted you to have, but he did not have enough money for the down payment. He asked us not to say anything to you and that he would pay us back over the next couple of months. Now you are telling me the two of you were not discussing buying another vehicle. I'm worried about his story. It's a bit sketchy, none of this makes any sense," Karen said.

Norma could hear the worry in Karen's voice. She thought about what the police sergeant said to her: Sometimes, people leave, and they don't want to go home. "None of this is making any sense to me either," she agreed. *Gaynard, WHERE ARE YOU, WHY DON'T YOU CALL?*

"Karen," Norma said, struggling to maintain her own composure, "this seems to become more of a mystery every hour. I will call you the moment I hear anything."

"Well, did you hear any of that?" Norma asked her mom and sister.

"We couldn't help but hear it," said Margie. "It sounded like Gaynard needed even more money."

"That's why none of this is adding up for me," said Norma. "We both have good jobs. We are making enough money to put some into a passbook savings account every month. I learned of a withdrawal from our savings account, which he said he loaned to a friend at work. He told me it would be replaced within a month or two. I should probably go to the bank on Monday and see if that account has other withdrawals that I don't know about. It's hard for me to believe that he took our change in that bottle, funds from our passbook savings, *and* borrowed from his parents. But I guess I would rather know that, than to think he is hurt somewhere and is not getting any help."

Their conversation would be interrupted another 5 or 6 times as word began to spread amongst friends and relatives. People were calling Norma to ask if there might be anything they could do.

"This is obviously quite stressful on you," said her mother. "How about if Margie or I, or both of us spend the night here so you don't go stir crazy? You'd have someone to talk to."

"That sounds like a good idea. I would like the company." Then she changed her mind. "On second thought, that might not be such a good idea. Tomorrow is Monday, and Gaynard will have to come home tonight to get ready for work tomorrow. If you are in the house, it would be awkward for me to talk to him about where he has been. And, I'm sure he'd be uncomfortable if either, or both of you, were here. I like the idea, but tonight would not be a good night to stay with me."

Margie and Inez reluctantly agreed. They stood up from the table and prepared to leave. The three of them hugged and agreed to call each other tomorrow.

Norma walked out into the back yard to begin picking up the sharp pieces of glass and the hundreds of pennies mixed amongst pieces of the broken bottle. She began by picking up the larger pieces of glass and putting them in the galvanized trash can she pulled out of the garage. She did not feel the sharp glass cut her right forefinger and index finger. A noticeable drop of blood on the concrete walkway drew her attention to her cut fingers. She ran cold water over the cuts and rubbed a little soap onto the wounds. The cuts on her fingers stung a bit when she cleaned them in the soapy water. She dried her hands and placed a band-aid over the cuts. Her cut fingers throbbed at the beat of her heart.

Then she went back outside and began picking up the pennies and putting them in a bowl. She picked one up and stared at it for a moment. She thought about where the penny might have been . . . how far did it travel before it ended up spilled outside her back door. Then she smiled, *it's funny what people can think of when they are going through a personal crisis.*

Around 4:00 p.m. there came another knock on her door, and the door opened. Her dad entered. Norma told him all that she knew about Gaynard being missing. She also told him that she suspected he might be spending more time at the race tracks than she realized.

"Norma," but before he could say another word, Norma interrupted.

"Dad, don't say that Gaynard might have run off with another woman, I've already heard that speculation from several sources."

Tom Malloy, opened his hands, palms up, in a gesture that suggested he wouldn't think of saying that. "Let's talk about this betting that he might be doing at the track. Do you have any inkling as to how much he might be betting on the horses? Any idea that he might have been getting into debt?"

"I accompanied him to the tracks on a few occasions. I did not suspect that something could be wrong. Gaynard did know a lot about the horses and the jockeys. He would try to show me how the odds work and what it means for a horse to place and show. I did not have much of an interest in that part of the racing. I would cheer for a horse because I liked its name. I remember Gaynard became quite excited one time that he took me to Santa Anita. Willie Shoemaker's name appeared on the horse and jockey line up that day. He told me that the horse can be a real good runner, but a jockey can make all the difference between winning and losing. Willie Shoemaker always seemed to be a winner."

"I haven't been to the horse races, but I know about Willie Shoemaker. He grew up about 10 miles from here in El Monte. He's a big supporter of kids sports all over the San Gabriel Valley. He has a sponsorship sign on the outfield fence at Bassett Little League Field where your cousin's played baseball," said Tom. "He is about as well-known as Sandy Kofax and Don Drysdale."

"Not everyone is a baseball fan like you, but we all know Sandy Kofax and Don Drysdale. We cannot turn the radio on without hearing about the Dodgers," she said.

"I am going to stop by the bank tomorrow and ask for our account history. I'm not sure if he has been hiding things from me, but I suppose I will know soon enough."

"You know that if you need any money to get by, your mother and I will help out," Tom said.

"Thank you," she said. "The first thing I want to do is sort through this nightmare and find out what happened to Gaynard and why he left. Or more importantly, how did he simply disappear? I am going to try and go to work tomorrow, if for nothing else, to get my mind away from all this worry. I'll contact the police department, if Gaynard does not return home tonight, and find out what else they might be able to do."

She asked her dad if he's been in contact with her brother, Mitchell.

Tom just shook his head, affirming that there has been no contact in a while.

Tom stood to leave and said, "You will have to consider all possibilities."

Norma shook her finger at him; a gesture that mostly implied, 'I don't want to hear it. "Don't go there, Dad!" she said.

Tom smiled, "I won't. Let us know what you find out tomorrow." He hugged his daughter and left.

Tom got home about an hour after Inez. When he entered the house, Inez asked him, "How do you think Norma is holding up? I offered to stay the night, but she thinks Gaynard might show up since he has to work tomorrow, and thought it to be awkward if Margie, or I, were there."

"That's a lot of worry, and stress, to put on one person. I am not sure what has happened to Gaynard, but I'm beginning to think it is a bit more troublesome than we realized. We haven't known him for a very long time, but what we do know is that it seems highly unlikely that he would take off for days, and tell no one of his whereabouts. It troubles me that Norma is so worried, and hurt. I feel awful for her. I'm not comfortable that she is home alone, but I don't know what we can do about it if she does not think one of us should be there."

"I tend to agree," Inez said. "Talking to Norma earlier today, I got the impression Gaynard might have incurred quite a bit of debt from betting. I find it hard to believe that he would not know how this is worrying his wife, his parents, and friends, by just leaving. He might be running from a problem that got out of control, unless something else happened. I don't want to worry unnecessarily. We need to be there for Norma and just take things one day at a time. Let's see what tomorrow brings."

"Yeah,' said Tom, "I can't help thinking about Mitchell through all of this. He has made himself absent from our lives for quite a while. Norma is struggling, and there doesn't seem to be anything we can do for her. Mitchell resists talking to us, or even letting us know where he's at. All this makes me feel so helpless."

He thought about how Mitchell drifted about and seldom left any information on where he would be staying. He began to withdraw from the family when he became a teenager and carried that over into his adult life. He got his dad's height, 6' 2" tall, thin, dark hair, and blue eyes. By all accounts he was a good-looking fella. Fitting in and sustaining a relationship has been elusive to him. He experienced every teenager's biggest fear; a bad case of acne that did not clear up until his early adult life. He may have been self-conscious about it, or even teased in school contributing to his withdrawal from people, even those closest to him.

He resisted relocating to California and entering a new school. Fitting in with a new crowd did not work out well for him. Mitchell pushed everyone close to him as far away as possible. He was not shy, but he withdrew from family contact, and that included his extended family, uncles, aunts, cousins, nieces and nephews. He effectively cut everyone out of his life. He would not even acknowledge the people around him.

Kids are perceptive and they seem to know when an adult is not friendly. Margie's kids were no different; they kept their distance. Mitchell never showed any signs of being a threat to them, he simply did not want anything to do with kids. His relationship between himself and his two sisters had been strained for many years.

"The answers will not come easy," Inez said. "My hope remains constant that Mitchell will come around, and realize how much we miss him.

I pray that Gaynard is all right, and there is an explanation for all of this. My instincts, however, tell me something more nefarious has happened. It's too unlikely that he would disappear without a trace, or anyone knowing of his whereabouts."

CHAPTER FOUR

A Hand Up

The alarm clock startled her awake. She still felt tired, but grateful for a little rest. The nightmare of the last several days came flooding back into her thoughts. She went into the living room, but noticed no sign that Gaynard returned home last night. Again, Norma looked out the front, and back doors, but did not see his truck at the house.

A hot cup of coffee, a shower, and she would go in to work. Upon entering the bathroom, she glanced in the mirror, *Oh no, my eyes! How bloodshot and swollen they are. I look like a walking mess!*

She pulled herself together somehow and headed off to work. Heading to work on Monday morning became the usual routine even though nothing seemed usual about today. The 12-to-15-minute drive to her office building, didn't hold the same level of awe. Springtime added new color to the Southern California landscape. Flowering plants and trees were blooming in vibrant colors; reds and whites were mostly prominent. Bougainvillea vines and Bottle Brush bushes were rich in red color, and the abundant citrus trees were bathed in brilliant white flowers. She always enjoyed the colorful landscape, but today it held less of an appeal.

Norma parked her car in the parking lot across the street from the title insurance office and walked in through the front doors. Her bubbly and energetic personality did not manifest itself as she entered the building. Avoiding eye contact, she went straight to her desk area and stood behind the desk for a few moments before sitting down.

One of her friends and co-workers, Nancy Brockus, noticed something amiss. She walked over to Norma's desk and asked, "Is everything alright?"

She did not look up at Nancy, but fought back the surge of hopelessness as she shook her head and said, "No . . . it's not."

Quietly, almost whispering so the other office staff could not hear, Nancy asked, "What's wrong?"

Norma looked up, her eyes welling with tears, she said, "My husband is missing. The police cannot find him, and none of our friends have seen, or heard, from him since Friday. I probably shouldn't have come to work today. I thought I could hold it together, but I couldn't be more wrong."

Nancy and the other office staff met Gaynard at various social events. Everyone in the title company office attended their wedding just seven months earlier. Nancy said, "If you need to go home, I can cover your work today. I will let Dave know that you have some personal business to attend to. He'll understand."

Norma thought she should be at home in case the police, or Gaynard, tried to reach her. She looked at Nancy and said, "I thought that by coming to work I could get my mind off of this problem, obviously I am not able to do that."

"Norma, go home. We will take care of things here. If you need anything, just give me a call."

Norma nodded, "Thank you, I hate to put any burden on you because of my problems."

"You would do the same for any of us."

Norma picked up her purse, slung it over her shoulder, came around the desk, and gave Nancy a big hug.

"If Dave asks why you needed to leave, can I share your concerns about Gaynard? He will want to know."

"Sure. It's not much of a secret anyway, my phone rang almost non-stop yesterday from friends and relatives wanting to know what happened."

"We are here for you, don't hesitate to call if we can help with anything, please," said Nancy.

On the drive home, she reflected on how much she appreciated Nancy. She thought about the gift the office personnel pitched in to buy them for a wedding present: a full eight-piece setting of China dishware. *It's a good feeling to have close friends when it seems like your whole world is coming apart.*

Norma remembered that when she began looking for part-time work, she read an ad in the San Gabriel Valley Tribune that a title company needed a full-time employee. She really did not want to work full time. Then she thought that maybe this would be a good time to save a little money. She could put her education on hold for six months or a year.

Nancy Brockus and the office manager, Dave, participated in the interview. They both told Norma that they were looking for someone with a little more experience. But Nancy recommended that the title company give Norma the opportunity. She did not disappoint them. Norma learned quickly and brought her youth and energy to the office atmosphere. Now, here she is in a personal crisis, and her office friend, and mentor, would be standing by to help. Norma felt blessed that people were there to help her. She also felt saddened that she might let people down that counted on her.

She thought, someone knows something about what happened to Gaynard, and I need to find out, now.

CHAPTER FIVE

Follow the Money

W hen Norma returned home, she called the Firestone Tire warehouse to see if her husband showed up to work that morning. John Hindson, answered the phone.

"Hi, John, this is Norma" . . . before she could say anything else. John interrupted her.

"Hey, Norma, tell me that Gaynard made it home, but he is a bit under the weather and you are calling in for him," he said.

She knew instantly that he did not show up for work. "Actually, I wanted to know if he reported to work, but it sounds like he did not."

John said, after a noticeable pause, "This does not sound good."

"When I spoke to you on Saturday, you said that Gaynard left work early the day before. He did not come home all weekend, and I thought that he would certainly show up for work today. Did he tell you why he left work early on Friday?"

"Oh, jeez, Norma. I am so sorry. He didn't say why he needed to leave early, he just mentioned that some kind of an emergency popped up and he needed to tend to it."

"No one has heard from him since Friday, and I just thought he wouldn't miss work, or notify you that he could not come in. Did you get a chance to see if he left work early over the past couple of months?"

"Norma, I'm afraid I opened a can of worms here. I'm relatively new at this supervisory role. I did inquire at the personnel office, and unfortunately, he has checked out early on many occasions. They allowed me to peruse his attendance record over the last six months. There is a concern that a pattern has developed. They said he has not reported in sick over the past three years, he never missed work. But starting six months ago, he would take an afternoon off maybe once a month. That has steadily increased to two and three times a month. I don't think it drew too much attention because we get paid by the hour, if you are not here, that's your loss.

"But we've become busier and busier. The work cannot go undone, so when someone is missing, someone else has to pick up the slack. That's become the issue. Gaynard's beginning to miss too much work. I'm sorry for having to tell you that."

A long silence occurred between them. Then Norma said, "John, I have to ask you a question, and I need for you to be painfully honest with me, will you do that?"

"Of course."

"Gaynard," she said, "told me that you borrowed some money from him a few weeks ago, maybe a month ago. What can you tell me about that? I'm not suggesting that you pay it back right now, I'm just trying to figure some things out."

John hesitated before answering. "Norma, I don't know where this is going, but I did not borrow any money from Gaynard. He borrowed money from *me*. It's been almost six weeks, maybe two months ago. He said he ran into some unexpected auto repairs and couldn't afford to get your car out of the shop until he paid the bill."

"How much did he borrow?"

"Three hundred dollars. Norma, what is going on? We've been friends for a while, tell me what I can do to help."

"There isn't anything you can do right now. But please contact me if you hear from him or if he shows up for work."

"I will. I'm concerned for both of you. Please don't hesitate to call me anytime. I'm here for you," he said and they ended the conversation.

What has my wayward husband been doing, and what has he gotten him-self into? I need to go to the bank and ask to see all the transactions in our joint accounts, so I'll know if he has withdrawn any more money!

Norma walked into the bank and noticed a line of people at the bank teller window. She looked around and saw a bank employee at a nearby desk. She approached the employee, introduced herself and explained why she came into the bank. The employee said she could help, and went to print a copy of Norma and Gaynard's transactions. She led Norma to a table where she could review them.

The transaction dates went back to the month just before they got married, when they merged their accounts. The first several months revealed everything that she expected, seen, and what she had been told—it all appeared normal, and they were doing fine. Their accounts were growing. Neither of them made any withdrawals from their savings account.

Then she came to the fourth month on the transaction sheet. There she noticed the first withdrawal for one hundred dollars. Two weeks later, she noticed the second withdrawal, and then a pattern of weekly withdrawals. By the sixth month of their marriage, Gaynard began pulling more money out of their account than they were depositing on a monthly basis. When she got to the day of his disappearance, their nearly three-thousand-dollar savings account dwindled to nothing on that Friday. She sat back in the chair feeling puzzled, confused and a bit angry. *What could he be doing? Why would he take all of our money and just leave? These are not the actions of a loving husband.* She knew there would be no answers until the two of them could talk.

CHAPTER SIX

Whereabouts Unknown

Norma left the bank, but did not go straight home. She could not wait any longer for the police to call her with updated news. She drove to the police station and asked for Sgt. Roseborough. When he came out to the foyer to meet her, she quickly identified herself as the person he spoke to last Saturday regarding her missing husband. She wanted to know if the police heard anything over the weekend.

"There have not been any reports submitted about your husband, or sightings of his vehicle. Have you been in contact with a Mrs. Karen Widick?"

"Yes, she is my mother-in-law."

He said, "She called here earlier this morning wanting to file a missing person's report on Gaynard Widick. I told her that you already informed us of his absence since last Friday, and that we were looking into it. I pretty much told her what I told you last week."

Norma thought, she is probably going as crazy as I am not hearing, or knowing, anything. She probably tried to reach me earlier today. I need to talk to her.

"I spoke to her yesterday. Karen is worried as much as I am. He wouldn't just take off like this."

"That's what I got from her, too."

"What should we do?" she asked. "It's driving us insane not to know anything about what happened to him. His work place told me earlier today that he has not shown up, nor has he contacted them. This is all so out of character for him."

"All of the local jurisdictions are aware of his disappearance. They will keep this on the daily briefing agenda with their patrol officers. They have a description of the vehicle, a picture, and description of Gaynard that you gave us. If either is spotted, we will make contact. There is no telling when that might happen," he said.

"Those of us who love him, and miss him the most, are starting to think the worst has happened."

"I would hope you don't go there. My suspicion is that he went on a binge, is sleeping it off, and probably a little embarrassed. I know it feels like you are playing a waiting game, but that is all you can do right now."

"I hope you are right about what happened," she said. "My imagination is getting the better of me. If he does not come home soon, real soon, tell me what you think could be the worst-case scenario."

The sergeant took a deep breath and let it out very slowly, "Mrs. Widick, your husband could have run afoul with some unsavory characters. Someone could have knocked him off, taken his truck out of state, or maybe even to Mexico. There is always the possibility that we will not see your husband, or his truck again. We have to keep looking and remain optimistic that we will find one, or the other, as that is more often the outcome."

She said, "He has been missing for three days now, and it is wearing me down not to think that the worst possible thing has happened to him. He has disappeared. I stopped by our bank before I came here. Our savings account has been depleted. Gaynard apparently withdrew all of our money last Friday, the day he failed to return home from work."

"Mrs. Widick, the report you filed last week regarding a potential burglary at your home and the money taken from the glass bottle led us to believe that someone you know took that money. Now it seems that someone may very likely be your missing husband. Especially now, since you are sure he cleaned out your savings account.

"I understand how hard this must be on you. The surrounding jurisdictions have been brought up to speed about this situation. The LAPD Missing Persons Division raised a concern about the money you reported missing when you filed the burglary report. We don't know the actual amount, but you have suggested that it could have been upwards of two grand. Now the discrepancy in your savings account—how much money do you estimate the amount withdrawn from that account?"

"A little over three thousand dollars."

"My suspicion is that he could have been involved with some loan sharks. Their practices are not always illegal, but people shouldn't be taking any loans from them. They can be ruthless if they loan you money, and you're late paying it back, or if you're short on your payment."

"I'm sorry," she said. "I've heard of loan sharks, but why do you think they could be involved?"

"Your husband seemed desperate to get his hands on money, lots of money, and quickly. He could have borrowed from a loan shark, someone that will provide quick cash. The borrower is sometimes in a panic, and agrees to unreasonable and extremely high interest rates. The re-payment time line is short. If he became involved with a loan shark and could not pay back the funds be borrowed, he could be in real trouble. I am not saying this is what happened to him. It's only one scenario based on what you described as uncharacteristic of him to just up and leave, coupled with a grab for money. Get some rest, Mrs. Widick, we will remain diligent in our search for him. We'll let you know the moment we learn something."

CHAPTER SEVEN

Struggling for Answers

Norma could not rest. Her thoughts kept her in a constant state of worry and fear that something awful has happened to her husband. She struggled through one more night of troublesome sleep.

Suddenly, and in a state of panic, she woke up. Her heart pounded hard in her chest, perspiring, and feeling disoriented. It took her a moment to collect her thoughts and be able to move. She sat up in bed, her heart still beating rapidly and wondered how a peaceful dream could become such a nightmare.

I remember dreaming about the things Gaynard and I liked to do. He enjoyed listening to Johnny Rivers, while I liked the Beach Boys. Sometimes we would host a party at our house and invite our friends. Everyone always seemed happy, especially Gaynard. Someone would throw a party somewhere every weekend while we were dating and during our marriage. She dreamt about the things they would do spontaneously; wake up on a Saturday morning and decide to go to the mountains, the beach, or an amusement park.

Then she found herself trying to steer her car in reverse. Going backwards down a hill and gaining speed. I hit the breaks to slow down but there were no breaks. The car kept going faster and faster. I knew it would fly off the roadway and over the cliff. Then I woke up in a panic.

What and awful nightmare, she told herself. The dream started out so relaxing, then everything became horribly out of control.

She put her feet on the floor and started to get out of bed. She sat on the edge of the bed for a while. *I can't eat. I can't sleep and when I do doze off, I wake up and my heart is pounding from nightmares. My life feels like I'm in that car and everything is careening out of control.* She rubbed her forehead, stood up and walked into the kitchen.

Another beautiful day in Southern California, the sunshine came streaming through the window. All the exhaustion over the past several days caught up with her. She felt grateful to get a little bit of shut-eye, even if she woke up to a nightmare. Her mind kept wandering and trying to sort out the problems that seemed to take a different turn day by day. What went wrong? Why didn't I see it? How is it going to be fixed? Is he alright?

Common sense told her that Gaynard would not have been sleeping off a binge for what is now the fourth day of his disappearance. She thought she needed to steel herself for that phone call, or knock on the door, informing her of something she didn't want to hear.

Norma decided to get dressed, and go into work. Staying around the house, waiting for the phone to ring became increasingly depressing. For four miserable days and nights, no one, including the police, knew where he might be, or if he could be injured, hospitalized, or worse. I shouldn't have asked the police for their opinion of a worst-case scenario; I can't get that conversation out of my mind. On the other hand, I know they are looking for him, and considering every possibility.

Norma arrived at work about half an hour later than her usual start time. When she walked in, a muffled hush fell over the office as her fellow workers stopped what they were doing for a brief moment. She felt embarrassed. Realizing that her fellow employees did not expect to see her back at work so soon. Her friend, Nancy, walked over to her desk and asked, "How are you doing today? Have you heard from Gaynard?"

Norma shook her head and looked up at her. "It's miserable and maddening to be at home, waiting for the phone to ring, expecting some kind of news, and hopefully good news. I need to be doing something to occupy my time, and take my mind off of the worries from which I don't seem to be able to escape."

Nancy put her hand on Norma's shoulder and said, "I can't imagine what you are going through. I did not expect you back until you heard from your husband. If you feel like you are under too much pressure, and need to leave, we will continue to cover everything for you."

"Thank you," she said solemnly and quietly. "And if I feel the need to leave, I will let you know."

Norma flinched every time the phone rang. She wondered if the police department might be calling her at work, or maybe one of her relatives, since my home phone would only ring and ring. Throughout the day, when the phone rang at her office desk, it would always be a client or someone inquiring about title insurance, escrow, or an update on the status of their policy.

At 5:00 p.m. she walked out of the office. Nancy walked with her and the two of them walked to Norma's car. Nancy said, "As difficult as this is for you, you did very well today. Call me if you need anything, and do not feel obligated to come into work tomorrow if you don't feel up to it."

On the way home, Norma stopped at a grocery store to pick up a few items. Feeling desperation as each hour passed, she knew the food at home began to run low. Sleep became a higher priority than eating and she could not get much of either and did not pay close attention to what needed to be replaced. Norma bought coffee, fruit, bread, cereal, and milk then drove home. Cooking a meal for one person did not appeal to her. She still did not feel hungry. *What a terrible way this is to lose weight, and I don't have any extra weight to lose.*

She walked in through the front door and set her groceries on the kitchen table. The phone rang and it startled her. She felt nervous and jumpy every time the phone rang. *How long would this go on?* She asked herself.

CHAPTER EIGHT

Difficult Questions

John Hindson contacted Norma and said, "I just wanted to let you know that we still have not heard from Gaynard here at work since last Friday."

Norma expressed her appreciation to John for keeping her informed. When she finished the conversation, and barely put the phone down, it rang again.

"Hello sweetheart," said her mother, "I tried calling you a few times today, but you did not answer. I thought you might have gone into work, and I did not want to bother you there."

Norma explained that she decided that morning to go to work to try and get her mind off of the situation. Inez put Tom on the phone, he just walked in after closing the business for the day.

He asked, "Hey sweetheart, how are you doing? Do you need anything?"

"Under the circumstances, I guess I am doing alright. You and mom will be the first to know if anything changes."

Around 6:00 p.m., Norma heard the front door open, and someone call her name. She recognized the voice of her sister. They agreed the day before that Margie would bring some dinner over this evening. Hamburgers and fries were on the menu. The two of them talked through the meal and discussed a variety of topics, including happier times when they were younger and lived in Iowa.

Margie asked her if she remembered chasing and catching fire flies in the summer months. Norma laughed recalling the little lightning bugs. Kids would run around holding mason jars collecting as many fire flies as they could. Then they would release them, and start the chase all over again. Right after the sun began to set, the fire flies appeared, a spectacular phenomenon. There were no fire flies in the San Gabriel Valley area.

The conversation inevitably came back to what happened, and where is he?

Norma said, "I thought about what may be a harsh reality today. The police want to be optimistic, and hope that he'll walk through the front door anytime. I know our seemingly happy life has been de-railed."

"What would you do if he walked in here right now?"

"I would be very happy that he is safe, and back home," Norma said.

"Then what?"

Norma thought about that for a moment. Gaynard would have to answer for all the hell he has put everyone through. "I'm not sure," said Norma. "Has Jimmy ever caused any doubt in your relationship, or violated your trust?"

"No, we seem to be on the same page for just about everything. We've never really talked about it, but he probably feels the same way I do. There is no room for one, or the other, to cause any grief, or doubt. We're committed to each other, and that is what's important. It has never been a concern. We don't agree on everything but we always know where the other one stands.

"I can tell you are hurt, Norma. I'm hurt for you, but I'm also angry. If he is not laid up somewhere and can't call, then in my view, he has failed to do his most important job: take care of you. And at that, he's failed miserably. I wouldn't tolerate it, and I wouldn't tolerate it for you," said Margie.

Norma stood up from the table, picked up the empty bag and papers from the fast-food dinner and walked over to the kitchen counter. She did not make direct eye contact with her sister then she said, "You know you might be the only person on the planet that can talk to me that way about my husband. If it were anyone else, I would probably tell them to leave. I don't have time to be angry right now. Yes, I'm hurt. I'm devastated. I thought Gaynard and I shared everything but he could not tell me what he's been up to. I'm hurt and I'm worried, and that is consuming me. It will probably give way to anger, but for now I can't find any."

"I know how you must feel," said Margie. "Our emotions are running in opposite directions. We all love Gaynard, but he has violated our trust on many levels. No one is going to tell you what to do, only you can make that decision. Whatever you decide to do, we will still be here for you—for both of you. But things will never be quite the same again. I don't think anyone will view him in the same way they did before he took off. He is not going to have a good reason why he left and certainly not this early in your marriage."

Norma knew that her young marriage hit a very rocky place. It would be difficult to patch things up and go back to being normal. Gaynard has caused a lot of unnecessary pain, and suffering. Norma did not want to experience this again. She glanced at her sister and said, "I suppose I have always been the eternal optimist. I know there will be some difficult times but we would weather them and move on together. How much worse can it get?"

"I would hope that's the case," said Margie. "I also think there will be a thread of suspicion about what he's doing when he can't explain his actions. We just don't know enough about him and his recent actions are not a good formula for a lasting, long, loving relationship."

Norma's eyes glistened as they welled up with tears. She said, "I am too exhausted and worried to be thinking about, or making decisions about, my future right now. I just hope nothing awful has happened to him, then we will see where things go."

The two sisters talked for hours until Margie said she needed to get back to Glendora to give Jimmy a break and put their kids to bed. They agreed to contact each other the next day.

Norma stayed up a little while longer, busying herself around the house, then tried to get some much-needed sleep.

Her thoughts drifted to the California coast. She could always find comfort in the beaches along the ocean front. She could be described as the personification of the Southern California beach girl. She recalled her frequent trips to the many coastal beach areas; Huntington, Laguna, Balboa, Seal Beach, and others as often as time would allow. The sound of the waves rolling onto the shoreline in a never-ending sequence, the call of the seagulls, and laughter of people. She loved to fill her senses by taking in the smell of the salt water, the scent of sunscreen lotion, and the warmth of the ever-present sun.

Sometimes, she went alone, but most of the time she could be found at the beach with her friends, or relatives. Sometimes while at the beach, she would run on the shoreline. It's more difficult to run on the sand than the asphalt or dirt tracks. She liked the area where the waves reached as far as they could onto the sand, and then retreated back to the ocean. That part of the beach always felt cool, and more solid under her feet.

She remembered when her Uncle Chuck, and Uncle Louie, would bring all the cousins, and neighborhood kids to the beach to go Grunion hunting. They would have a campfire, and usually arrive between 9:00 p.m. or 10:00 p.m. Roasting hot dogs became a high priority on the agenda. Long after the sun would set, sometimes as late as midnight, flashlights would be brought out, and shined on the shoreline. The Grunion would get washed up on shore by the hundreds of thousands. They would shimmer in the light of a full moon. Then everyone would grab a bucket and gather up as many Grunion as they could until the tiny fish returned to the vast ocean, disappearing from the shoreline.

Grunion are small fish that swarm the coastal beaches to spawn. More specifically, the sandy beaches. They bury their eggs in the sand. Grunion are edible, but the fun for Norma would not be in the catching and eating the Grunion, the fun came in the event itself. It seemed like an all-night adventure, but the Grunion were not on the beaches all night. The tiny fish might wash up on the shore for one, maybe three hours, and then they were gone. Another challenge was trying to avoid getting too wet from the waves that kept rolling in. More often than not, the tiny fish would be poured out of the buckets and back into the surf. It is a fun catch and release event.

She reminisced about other times when she strolled along the beach, watching the sun set beneath the horizon over the Pacific Ocean. She would watch other people walking along the shoreline, sometimes there would be a couple of dogs running around them. She found it entertaining to watch the dog owners pick up a stick, or piece of driftwood, and toss it into the breaking waves. The dogs would bound into the water, retrieve the stick and run back to their owners expecting them to throw the stick again. She appreciated the Southern California coastline, it's always beautiful, and it never disappointed her. Daytime, evening, night, and even when there would be an infrequent rain, the beaches were spectacular.

She slept most of that night on the couch.

The next day, Wednesday, moved by painfully slow. No word came from the Police Department, or from any friends that might have heard from her husband.

Then, early Thursday morning the phone rang. *It's too early for the phone to be ringing*

CHAPTER NINE

Long Way from Home

S he woke up, startled. Norma glanced at the clock on the night stand next to the bed, it read 4:10 a.m. Her heart pounded. She asked herself, *Am I dreaming, or is this horrible reality still continuing? It's too early for anyone to be calling. Oh God, I hope it is not bad news about Gaynard. Maybe it's him.* Suddenly fully awake, she raced into the living room.

Norma picked up the phone, and in a weak voice said, "Hello?" She could not quite find her voice after being awakened.

"Hello, my name is Detective Frieler, I am calling from the Las Vegas Police Department. I am sorry to bother you at this hour, but I am hoping to talk to Gaynard Widick, is he there?"

Norma's head began pounding with every beat of her heart. "I am Mrs. Widick, Gaynard is my husband. He is not here. He has been missing since last Friday. Why are you wanting to talk to him?"

"A vehicle has been reported as abandoned at one of our hotels. The license plate number: California MHD 923 and the registration on the vehicle led me to the address in Alhambra, California. I secured the phone number to this address after a registration search."

"Is he there? Is he in Las Vegas?" she asked.

"It appears that he has been here. He checked into a hotel late last Friday night, and then checked out on Monday, but he did not take his vehicle. He left it in the parking lot. Hotel security called a local tow company and they currently have in their vehicle yard. We are going to have it the vehicle transferred to our impound yard. Towing companies are required to notify us whenever they pick up an abandoned vehicle." He added, "We did receive a bulletin from the Alhambra Police Department earlier this week about a missing person and a pickup truck. The one removed from the hotel parking lot matches the description of the truck. I'm trying to find the owner, and you are telling me he is not at his residence, and has not been there since last Friday, is that correct?" he asked.

The pounding of Norma's heart became deafening in her ears. She found it difficult to speak. "Yes, my husband, Gaynard, has been missing since last Friday." Norma could not find her voice; her thoughts raced faster than she could gather words to ask any questions.

"We are checking other hotels to see if he registered at another site, but left his truck where they found it at the Golden Nugget Hotel. So far, we have come up with nothing regarding a Gaynard Widick checking into another hotel. The truck will be held in our impound yard until we can locate the owner. If you would like to come get it, we would release it to you, his wife."

"Yes," said Norma in a voice that sounded weaker than her hello. "I will come and get the truck." She wanted to scream from the anxiety of worry, and fear, which she felt like it crept into and now occupied every corner of her life. She managed to ask the detective, "Can I get a phone number where I can reach you if I have any questions, right now I cannot find my thoughts. I will call you back this morning, and let you know when I will be traveling to Las Vegas to get the vehicle."

The detective gave her his number and said, "I know how difficult this must be. Please accept my apologies for calling at such an hour. If you need any assistance, call this number at any time."

"Thank you," said Norma and hung up the phone.

She glanced at the clock, it read 4:30 a.m. She knew she could not go back to bed; sleep would be impossible. She wanted to talk to someone. *Who should I call at this hour?* She debated whether or not to call her parents, maybe her sister. She knew that whoever she called would be startled to hear the phone ringing this early. It might even wake everyone up at Margie's including Jimmy and their three kids. She picked up the phone and dialed her parents' number. She counted the number of rings, ten . . . eleven . . . twelve, then her dad answered the phone.

"Dad," she said, "I did not want to call you this early and wake you up, but I just got a call from the Las Vegas Police Department. They found Gaynard's truck, but not Gaynard."

"Norma," he said, "First of all, you can call me anytime of the day or night. Tell me what the LVPD told you."

"Not much," she said as she struggled to hold back her emotions. Then she said, "He checked into a hotel last Friday night, and checked out on Monday. His truck has been impounded, and they want to know if I want to come and get it. I told them I did."

They talked for a while, and Tom said, "I think it would be best if you came over here. We can talk more about getting the vehicle. I don't want you driving right now, so I will come and get you."

Norma started to protest but acquiesced to the idea, she needed to talk and sort things out. This would be as good a time as any.

Her mother made coffee, while Tom went to pick up their daughter. Tom, Inez, and Norma sat around the kitchen table and talked for hours. At 8:00 a.m., the phone rang, Inez answered it.

Margie said, "I tried calling Norma to make plans for this afternoon before she went off to work, but she must have gone in to work because she did not answer."

Inez said, "She's here. The police found Gaynard's truck in Las Vegas. We are talking about driving over there to get it. They still do not know of Gaynard's whereabouts."

Margie said, "I will be there as soon as I can, I'll ask Jimmy to get the two older kids ready for school, and I'll bring the baby."

When Margie arrived, the four of them discussed everything that happened in the past week. Their fear that something awful has happened to Gaynard began to dominate their thoughts.

Margie asked, "How long ago did you talk to Gaynard's Parents?"

"Night before last," Norma said.

"I'll call them for you and bring them up to date on this latest information," Margie said, and slipped away into the living room to use the phone.

Norma got up and followed Margie. "I should probably make the call. His parents are going to have a lot of questions. How about if you open the blinds and curtains to allow some light in here."

Margie raised her eyebrows and glanced at her sister. Lately, their dad insisted that the blinds and drapes be kept closed. He expressed more than a few times that he believed someone is watching the house. No one, Inez or his daughters, could find any basis for his suspicion. Margie opened the drapes and blinds.

Norma told Gaynard's parents the LVPD does not know where he is, only that he allegedly checked into and out of the hotel where they found the truck.

The in-laws asked a lot of questions, but Norma did not have the answers. She understood their concerns and their worries about their son. No one in the family could escape the anxiety from what could have happened to Gaynard. She told his parents that she and her mom and dad were talking about going to Las Vegas to retrieve the vehicle. She said she would let them know of any plans they make regarding that trip.

Floyd Widick said, "Karen and I would like to go along on that trip to get the truck."

Norma thought this to be a good idea and said, "Let me talk that over with my parents, and I'll get right back to you."

Tom and Inez were planning on making the trip to get the truck. However, having Gaynard's parents go along would work out very well.

Inez, looked at Norma and said, "Let's make it a mother/daughter road trip. We have not been able to do that in quite a while, and it always seemed like so much fun, just the two of us. The Widick's can join us on the drive to Vegas and then you and I can stay overnight." Inez knew that she could not relieve Norma of her burden or the feelings that were wearing her down. She thought that the two of them could enjoy one another's company and lessen the deepening anxiety.

Tom concurred. He wanted to be there every moment for his daughter, but he also realized that this would be a good time for mother and daughter to spend some quality time together.

Norma spoke to the Widick's and asked, "How soon can you leave? I would like to leave tomorrow, Friday morning."

Floyd said, "That will work just fine. We will see you and Inez tomorrow morning."

Norma, contemplating the travel plans, looked up at the ceiling, she rolled her eyes and said loudly, "Oh No! I forgot to go into work this morning. I haven't contacted anyone. The call from the LVPD completely distracted me!"

She took several deep breaths, then went to the phone to check in at her office. Nancy Brockus answered. Norma gave Nancy a brief update about the status of Gaynard's vehicle being found in Las Vegas, and apologized for completely forgetting about checking in at work.

Nancy said, "The office atmosphere has been a bit on the worrisome side, since we did not hear from you this morning. It is certainly understandable how it slipped your mind. You have a lot going on right now."

Norma said, "We are planning to leave first thing tomorrow morning to go get the truck. My mom and I will stay overnight, and drive my car back on Saturday. I'll be in the office on Monday morning."

Nancy said, assuringly, "Don't worry about work, drive safely, and we will see you on Monday morning with hopefully good news."

Tom told Norma and Margie, "Your mother and I have been trying to contact your brother to find out if he has heard anything. He doesn't stay in one place very long. We have left messages for him to contact us. But so far, there's been no word from him. He hasn't left a forwarding address, or phone number, either.

Norma thought to herself, it's probably better that Mitchell could not be reached. She wasn't sure what help he would be, and their relationship had been strained for as long as she could remember. She did not say anything because she knew both of her parents were distraught over Mitchell's troublesome behavior.

Margie did not say anything either. She and Norma shared the same opinion; Mitchell's presence would probably make matters worse.

Mitchell chose one of life's paths that would cause him to spiral into an abyss that he would not be able to get out of. Tom and Inez were vaguely aware of what he had been doing, but they were not aware of the extent of the trouble he so easily slipped into, or the secret he kept from his parents. Shortly after high school, Mitchell moved out of his parents' house. When Inez cleaned up his bedroom to get it ready for her grandkids to spend the night, she found stacks of pornographic magazines. They heard, but could not confirm, that he took a job working at one of the porn shops in downtown Los Angeles.

CHAPTER TEN

Road Trip

The drive from the Alhambra/San Gabriel area to Las Vegas is about four-and-a-half hours. The four of them, her mom, Gaynard's parents, and Norma could take Norma's car. She drove a 1957 Chevy that could accommodate them. Norma would spend Thursday night at her parent's house, and she and her mom would pick up the Widick's around 9:00 a.m. the next morning.

Inez told her traveling companions that she and Tom stopped in Las Vegas on a trip they took on the way to Iowa when visiting relatives two years earlier. She added that Norma did not make that trip and has not been to Las Vegas all the while she lived in California.

She and her mother would spend Friday night at the Flamingo Hotel/Casino. They planned to enjoy the bright lights, have a nice dinner, maybe take in a show. They would get a good night's sleep, and then drive back home.

Inez and Norma would talk to the LVPD detective, Harold Frieler, when they arrived in Las Vegas to get any more details that the detective might have learned about Gaynard's truck being abandoned in Las Vegas.

The foursome left for Las Vegas Friday morning shortly after 9:00 a.m. Norma left a message for Detective Frieler, updating him on her Friday afternoon arrival and she would contact him as soon as they arrived in Las Vegas.

Mr. and Mrs. Widick were not planning to stay the night in Las Vegas. They would get the truck out of the impound yard and drive it back home the same day.

Norma's 1957 Chevy Belair, 4-door sedan, automatic transmission, and small V-8 engine provided a comfortable ride for the four adults. Air conditioning units were not yet a standard feature in most cars, and this one did not have it. The time of year, late March, made it easier to travel without air conditioning. The outside daytime temperature would not rise high enough to make it feel like a necessity to have air conditioning. Most automobiles included a 'wind wing' on the front passenger, and driver side doors. The small wind wing windows could be pushed open to allow air circulation into the vehicle without having a window rolled down, allowing a light breeze into the car and reduce outside road noise.

The road to Las Vegas from Los Angeles traveled on Interstate 15. Several years earlier the highway became part of the nation-wide interstate system, a project launched by President Eisenhour in 1956.

Inez drove the car the entire route. She knew Norma would not be up to the task, and Mr. Widick planned on driving straight back home as soon as they got the truck. They stopped a couple of times along the route to get a cold soda, and another time to get some gas and clean the bugs off the windshield. They found a small diner at the gas station where they ate a light lunch and then got back on the road. They traveled most of the way through the flat, sparse, dry Mojave Desert.

The four traveling companions tried to keep the mood, and conversation, as upbeat as they could. They talked about a variety of topics.

Inez and the Widick's were all about the same age.

Inez said, "I fondly remember the one-room school house I attended. One teacher instructed kids in grades 1 through 8. Most of the school buildings in rural America were heated by a pot-bellied wood stove. Drinking water would be hauled in from the pump outside of the school house. There were no restrooms, but the outhouses were just outside the building. One-room school houses were quite common in rural America. The more populated areas obviously needed larger school systems."

The Widick's laughed and said, "Our experience did seem a little different. We did not have a pot-bellied stove for heat. We attended school in the warmer Southern California climate."

Inez said, "I met Tom at a high school social. He attended the Catholic school in our home town of Fort Dodge, Iowa. I attended the public school.

Every year, the two schools hosted a social dance. We met my sophomore year, Tom's junior year."

Inez, Floyd and Karen all graduated from high school during the Roaring 20's. They laughed about their clothes and dancing that they did during that time of national prosperity.

"Do you remember the devastating effect of the Great Depression that hit the country and the world in 1929, at the height of the Roaring 20's?" asked Inez.

"That is something our generation will never forget. The Great Depression brought a lifestyle change that impacted just about everyone in the country. It lasted right up to World War II," said Karen. "When did you and Tom get married?"

"1932—three years into the depression." They talked about what a difficult time that had been. They reminisced about the things they experienced and lived through: two world wars, a worldwide pandemic—the Spanish Flu, two U.S. Presidents that died in office, and a third one assassinated in Dallas, Texas while campaigning for re-election.

The JFK assassination dominated most of their talking. Even Norma weighed in on that discussion. She said, "It seems like it happened just yesterday, even though it has been four months ago just before Thanksgiving. That moment, that day, will probably always be remembered. Millions and millions of people were devastated. The insurance office closed early that day. I think a lot of businesses closed early when the news broadcasted the president's sudden and shocking death."

The conversation of the four travelers would inevitably wind its way back to the reason they were going to Las Vegas—what happened to Gaynard, where did he go, and why, and how he just disappeared without any communication?

Norma turned slightly in her seat, her back against the passenger door so she could see her in-laws. She said, "I have talked to everyone I can think of that we knew, and no one has heard from him, or at least that's what they told me."

"I've called everyone I can think of that Gaynard knew in high school, even his childhood friends, all of our relatives, and none of them have heard from him," said Karen.

Norma added, "The police suggested that he could be in some kind of trouble that might involve a loan shark. They said this fits the profile of someone desperately needing money."

Floyd said, "That's the difficult part of this whole thing. He has to know that if he needed any help, we would be there for him. It never crossed our minds when he borrowed money from us for a car purchase that it wasn't true. It is disturbing he hid something from us, and that he did not have enough trust to tell us he might be in some kind of trouble."

They talked about the possibility of gambling being the cause of his disappearance. Norma said, "He has been spending more time than I realized at the Santa Anita Park race track. It just seemed like any entertainment event, only this one involved watching the horses run. I cannot imagine that it could cause trouble."

"Neither can we," said Karen. "We've known him all his life. We raised him. Nothing that has happened in the past week is adding up to make any sense to us."

Norma sensed the conversation going dark. The stress of the past week wore thin on her nerves. Gaynard's actions were having a negative and worrisome impact on everyone in the car. She decided that there would not be a better time than now to put it all out in the open. "Let's address the elephant in the room. Could there be another woman involved? I still do not think so. His leaving like he did, his truck being found, and still no sign of him does not allow for another woman to be a part of this mystery."

"Oh, I never thought there might be anyone else involved," said Karen apologetically. "Gaynard's feet did not touch the ground when he started dating you. Happy would be understating how he felt, and we were happy for him. You are the best thing that has happened to all of us. He loves you, and only you. I am sure of that."

Inez looked in the rear-view mirror and saw Karen's eyes looking back at her. She silently said, "Thank you."

Norma did not hold the same level of confidence. She kept hearing the words of the police sergeant: "Gaynard might not want to come home, and there is nothing we can do about that." Her mother and sister suggested there might be another woman involved. As much as Norma did not want to believe it, she knew she must face the fact that something must be very wrong in their marriage. She might have to carry on alone, without her handsome and fun husband. She thought, if I have to move on by myself, I would prefer to do that knowing that Gaynard is all right, that nothing terrible has happened to him. She kept her thoughts to herself.

The mood became a little lighter, and the conversation made the trip seem shorter. The anxious foursome pulled into the City of Las Vegas at 2:30 p.m., a little more than 5 hours after they left San Gabriel that morning.

Inez asked, "Is anyone hungry? Should we get something to eat, or go straight to the P.D. to get the truck?" They agreed to go to the P.D. and get the truck, then they would think about eating.

Upon arrival at the police station, they all entered the building. Norma walked up to the counter and asked to see Detective Frieler.

The detective, tall and smartly dressed, entered the lobby area. He greeted them and said, "I am Detective Frieler, it's a pleasure to meet you."

Norma nodded and introduced herself, her mother, and then Mr. and Mrs. Widick. "Floyd and Karen will be driving the truck back to Alhambra this afternoon. My mom and I will be spending the night here in Las Vegas."

Detective Frieler said, "Let's go into our conference room to talk. Can I get you anything to drink?" Before anyone could decide, the detective stepped into a side room and brought out four cups of water.

After they were all seated, he said, "I don't have any new information on Gaynard's whereabouts. We are still checking the other hotels, but so far, nothing."

"Did you find anything in the truck that might give us an idea of where he is?" Norma asked.

"Well, we searched through the vehicle, but found nothing that gave us any clues to where he might have gone. Both doors were locked on the truck but the towing company drivers have been taught how to open a door using an access tool without breaking the windows. I hope you brought a spare key to start the engine so you can drive the vehicle back home."

"Luckily, I gave a spare key to my father-in-law before we left this morning."

"Good. Other than what I spoke to you about on the phone, there has been nothing else that popped up. Our patrol division has been instructed to detain Gaynard if they come in contact with him. We want to make sure that he is all right.

"We should probably head over to the impound yard now, so we can get the vehicle out before they close. There will be some paper work for you to fill out. Also, I would like you to go through the truck and see if there is anything you might notice to help us track his whereabouts. The impound yard is only a few blocks away. It is probably quicker if we walk there. Is everyone up for that?" They all agreed.

Once they reached the impound yard, Norma filled out the release papers for the truck, and started to pay the impound fees. Floyd interrupted her by insisting that he pay the cost for having the truck released.

One of the workers brought the truck around to the front of the impound yard, and the four of them went through it thoroughly. They looked under the seat, behind the seat, above the sun visors, and in the glove box. They found nothing that could give them any idea why Gaynard came to Las Vegas or where he might have gone. By 4:30 P.M. that afternoon they effectively scoured the truck inside and out.

Inez asked again if anyone else might be getting hungry.

Mr. Widick said, "We would rather get on the road for the drive back, it will be 9:00 or 10:00 p.m. by the time we get back home, if we don't have too many stops. If we get hungry, we'll stop along the way." The four of them said their goodbyes, and Mr. and Mrs. Widick started back to Southern California.

Norma, Inez, and the detective walked back to the police station where they left Norma's car. "Where will you be staying tonight in case I need to contact you?' he asked.

Norma replied, "We will be at the Flamingo Hotel. We have not checked in yet, so we don't have a room number to give you."

"I know the hotel, and I have the front desk number. I can ask them to transfer a call to your room. I will let you know if anything new materializes. Enjoy your stay, I wish it could have been under more pleasant circumstances."

The next call the detective received would shock even the most seasoned officers.

Photo source: South Point Gallery
Flamingo Hotel – circa 1950's

CHAPTER ELEVEN

Trunk Key

Norma and Inez made reservations at the Flamingo Hotel, often referred to by its nickname: The Pink Hotel. They pulled up in front of the lobby area where a valet offered to park their car, and bring in their luggage. Inez said, "Thank you very much, but we have not checked in yet."

The valet said, "That's OK. You go ahead to the check-in desk, and I'll unload your luggage and bring it to you. One of the bellhops will follow you to your room and bring your luggage."

Within moments of Norma and Inez reaching the check-in desk, the valet showed up and said, "There is a minor problem. When I put the key in the trunk of the car to get your luggage, it broke off. I could not get the trunk open, and your luggage is still inside the trunk of the car."

The front desk clerk asked, "Would you like for me to call a locksmith?"

"Of course," came Norma's reply. "We don't have any clothes, or toiletry items, everything is locked up in the trunk."

The clerk pulled out a phone book and began contacting locksmiths she found in the yellow pages. She made several calls; most lock and key shops were closed by 5:00 P.M. Finally, she got an answer at one of the shops. She explained the problem and the locksmith said that he would wait for them if they wanted to bring the car to him. He said he would be there a little while longer because he needed to finish some additional work.

Inez agreed to that. The desk clerk wrote down the address and handed it to her stating that the shop is about a mile from the hotel.

Norma and Inez finished checking into the hotel. They walked up to their room to take a quick look, and then headed back to their car.

They arrived at the locksmith shop close to 6:00 p.m.

They found the door to the building locked. Looking through the glass window they could not see anyone in the building. They knocked on the glass and pretty soon a man came out of a back room and opened the door.

He said, "I am sorry about that. We typically close at 5:00 p.m. I knew you were on your way, but I locked the door so I would not get any late walk-in traffic. Thanks for knocking, I might have been pre-occupied putting together some supplies for another job and did not hear you drive into the parking lot. What can I do for you?"

Inez explained the problem and showed the locksmith the broken key in the trunk lock.

He said, 'It is going to be dark soon, so I will pull the vehicle into the shop and work on it where there is better lighting. You can wait here, or do you have something else to do?"

"How long do you think this will take?" asked Inez.

"Give me a couple of hours."

"We are both hungry, can you suggest a place where we can get something to eat?"

"The Sands Hotel and Casino is within walking distance; they have a rather nice restaurant and the food is pretty good there." He gave them directions to the Sands. "Write down your names for me and I will call over there to the restaurant to let you know when your car is ready. I am going to grab a bite to eat also, finish up what I started doing before you got here, and then I will start on your car."

Norma and Inez walked to the Sands Hotel and Casino. They sat down in a booth and sipped on a cup of coffee while they looked over the dinner menu. They found some levity in their circumstance. "What are the chances of a key breaking off in the trunk of the car at the end of a long drive," Inez asked?

"Or not having a change of clothes and being unable to clean up and go see a few things we came here to see. At least we didn't run out of gas and have to hitch hike somewhere to fill up a gas can, or change a flat tire," responded Norma.

They laughed and then ordered their meals. Inez informed the waitress that they were expecting a call from the nearby locksmith and gave her their names.

"Mom," Norma said, "I'm sorry that you have to go through this too."

Inez smiled at her daughter and said, "You don't need to apologize to me. That's what family does, we want to be there for one another. I want to be here with you. Everyone will experience some rough spots in their life. There are good times and there's bad times. We'll get through this and we'll get through it together."

"Thanks mom, I do appreciate you being here. I really do."

They talked throughout dinner. When the waitress came by to refill their coffee cups, Inez asked if there were any calls for them from the locksmith shop.

"No," said the waitress. "Would you like for me to call over there and check on the status of your vehicle?"

"If you don't mind, I would really appreciate that."

The waitress came back and said, "I let the phone ring for quite a while, but no one answered."

"The shop is closed for the day, and I doubt that he will answer the phone. He said he would call over here when he finished. I suppose we could walk back and see if the lock has been repaired," said Inez.

The two women paid for their dinner and walked back to the locksmith shop. They found it to be locked up tight just like their earlier visit. They needed to knock on the window to get the attention of the locksmith like they did earlier that evening.

He apologized for the inconvenience and told them he is just now getting around to working on their car. He said it might be another hour.

Norma looked at her wristwatch, just past 8:00 P.M. She and her mother discussed waiting or walking back to the Sands. They decided on the latter. The locksmith said if they were going back to the Sands, he would call over there and have them paged as soon as the car is ready.

The first hour went by quickly. They played a few of the one-arm bandits then went to the restaurant for some dessert. Two hours passed. Then they heard their names over the pager system. They walked up to the front desk. The clerk said she just heard from the locksmith; their car is ready to be picked up.

Nearly 10:30 p.m. and the two women were feeling tired. They were able to grab a taxi just outside of the casino to take them back to the locksmith shop. They noticed their car parked out in front of the shop in the parking lot area. They felt bad and frustrated at the same time. They appreciated the locksmith working late to help them out, but they dropped their car off over four hours ago.

By the time they paid their bill for the key lock replacement and new key, they noticed the time to be just after 11:00 p.m.

CHAPTER TWELVE

Dark Desert Night

Inez got into the driver's side of the car, and Norma got into the front passenger seat. Inez started the car, put it in drive, began to move it forward towards the boulevard.

"I'll be so glad to kick off my shoes and flop back on a Pink Flamingo bed," said Norma.

"Me too, I'm exhausted. This has been a very long day."

Suddenly, and surprisingly, a man appeared in the back seat. He apparently got into the car when left unattended in the locksmith parking lot. He managed to hide by lying down on the floor in the back of the car.

Startled, Inez hit the brakes. The darkness in the car prevented her from seeing the person in the back seat very clearly. Glancing several times in the rear-view mirror, she turned her head toward the back seat and yelled, "Who are you? How did you get in here? Get out of this car, now!"

The man grabbed her by the hair on the back of her head and pulled back hard. He pointed a handgun at the side of Inez's head. She groaned in pain as he tightened his grip on her hair forcing her head backwards. He yelled, "Drive, and do what I tell ya to do."

Inez screamed, "RUN NORMA, RUN!"

The man tightened his grip. He pulled harder on Inez's hair, yanking her head backwards, she yelled in pain. "Open that door, and I'll shoot both of ya," he pointed the gun at Norma. "Now drive."

Norma hesitated to open the door and flee. She glanced at her mother. She could see the pain on her face as the man continued to grip and pull on her hair. She noticed blood trickling from the cut on her mother's nose where he pushed her head forward, hard onto the steering wheel.

Inez resisted the man's grip. He yanked harder on her hair. Norma could see the expression of fear and pain on her mother's face.

Norma did not run; she took her hand off the door handle.

"Drive," the man shouted at Inez. She slowly removed her foot from the brake pedal. The car moved forward and she steered it onto the boulevard. She turned right, heading south. Within minutes they were on the outskirts of town.

Five miles later, they were outside the city of Las Vegas. No more lights, no buildings, no houses, nothing but the headlights of the car hitting the pavement in front of them. A clear desert sky and its millions of stars could not overcome the darkness, total darkness. *Where are we going? What does he want?*

Maintaining the tight grip on her hair, the man told her to drive until he tells her to stop. Fearing for her daughter's safety, Inez tried to think of how they could escape their captive. She could not piece together a plan of escape.

PART TWO

CHAPTER THIRTEEN

Stake Out

Don Long worked the graveyard shift at the pay-to-park lot in downtown Las Vegas. He noticed a 1957 Chevy, 4-door sedan pull into the lot. People were coming and going all hours of the day and night. He watched the vehicle arrive around 1:00 a.m., pass the entrance booth, and the driver take a ticket from the single arm gate that raised up to let the vehicle enter. Don saw the car pull into an available space. He noticed one person exit the car, and walk in the direction of the adjacent hotel/casino.

Don walked through the lot hourly to make sure the parked vehicles displayed a ticket stub on their dash, so the attendant knew the vehicle driver did not sneak into the lot. Shortly after the '57 Chevy entered the parking area; Don Long made his rounds. Everything looked normal. As he began walking back to the entry booth, he strolled by the passenger side of the Chevy. A broken window caught his eye.

He pulled a flashlight from his coat pocket and shined it into the car. He saw broken shards of glass on the front seat, and floor of the vehicle. He noticed dark colored stains on the front seat, and thought that it might be spilled alcohol. He shined the light into the back seat and saw a small duffle bag and a crumpled-up shirt. He became alarmed when his flashlight revealed a hand gun inside the duffle bag. Hurriedly, Don went back to the booth and did not check the car for any further tell-tale signs of possible foul play. He picked up the phone, and dialed hotel security.

"I have a vehicle that entered the lot about 20 to 30 minutes ago. You might want to send someone over to take a closer look at the car. It looks a bit suspicious," Don said.

"What do you have?" asked the shift operator.

"A broken window, glass in the car, stains on the seat, and a hand gun. Maybe it's nothing, but I just thought you should check it out."

"We will have someone over there shortly. Will you be at the entry booth so you can show them where the car is parked?" asked the operator.

"Yes, I will."

One of the security guards showed up to meet Don Long about ten minutes after the call. They walked over to the parked car and examined it again. The broken window and gun in the back seat gave them cause to contact the police department. The security guard went back to the booth, called the hotel operator, and asked her to call the Las Vegas Police Department regarding a suspicious car. He would wait for the police at the parking lot entrance.

Twenty minutes later, an LVPD police car arrived and two officers stepped out of the vehicle. Don Long and the security guard led the officers to the '57 Chevy.

The officers noticed stains on the windshield, dashboard, and the seat. They could not tell if the stains were mud, spilled alcohol, or possibly blood. One of the officers pulled on the passenger side front door, it opened. The broken window on the door made it impossible to secure the car. They put on gloves, and pulled the duffle bag from the back seat. The gun in the bag revealed two spent bullet casings from the .38 caliber Colt revolver. The chamber held six bullets; four were live; two were used. They pulled the crumpled shirt from the back seat and examined it under their flashlights. Severely stained but they could not determine what the stains were from.

One of the officers shined his flashlight on the vehicle license plate— California plates JIE 124. Then he looked at the registration attached to the steering column and made note of the address in Alhambra, California. He also made note of the name on the vehicle registration.

The officers radioed back to the LVPD dispatcher. They requested that a supervisor respond to the parking lot.

Sergeant Schenkenberger soon arrived at the site. After being apprised of what the two officers found, he decided to pull back from the vehicle to wait and see if the driver returned for the car. The sergeant instructed the officers to move their patrol vehicle, so it would not be noticeable. Then he radioed back to the station to inform the dispatcher that he and the two officers would be setting up a surveillance of the car in the parking lot. He knew this would be a long shot to wait for someone to return and retrieve the vehicle. The sergeant believed the car to be stolen and possibly connected to a crime. He also knew that the perpetrator may have stolen the vehicle, used it to get where it's at, and more than likely did not plan on returning to get the car. The two officers took up positions in the shadows of the lights and the buildings, so they could not be easily spotted. Then the waiting game began.

More than an hour passed, a man and a woman walked through the parking lot in the direction of the Chevy. They went by the car and entered into a different vehicle parked several stalls away. This happened again and again, a false alarm every time someone entered the parking lot.

Then a lone man approached the vehicle. He appeared to be about 5 feet, 9 inches in height, thinning hair, and unshaven. He wore a dark colored button up shirt. The moment his hand reached for the driver side door handle, Sgt. Schenkenberger stepped in from the shadows and said, "Excuse me, sir, is this your car?"

The man looked at the sergeant, then glanced back over his shoulder and saw a uniformed officer standing directly behind him. The man said, "What is this all about?"

"Sir, is this your car?" the sergeant repeated.

"No, it belongs to my girlfriend."

"I would like to see some identification, yours, and the registration for the car, please."

The sergeant noticed the man to be irritated and suspected he is likely intoxicated. The third officer positioned himself so the man could not access the vehicle where the gun still sat on the back seat of the car in the duffle bag.

The man hesitated to respond. He glanced back and forth between the sergeant and the officer standing behind him. His hand still holding on to the car door handle.

"What is this all about?" the man demanded again.

"We just need to ask you some questions. Identification, please," said the sergeant.

The man then reached into his back pocket, and pulled out a wallet. He handed the officer his driver's license.

Studying the driver's license, the sergeant asked, "Does your girlfriend live in the Las Vegas area?"

"Yes," the man replied.

"What is her name?"

"Why? That's none of your damn business."

"Sir, what is your girlfriend's name and address?" asked the sergeant, in a tone that sounded like more of a demand, than a question.

The man did not respond, he just glared at the sergeant.

"Your driver's license says that you are a resident of Portland, Oregon. Is that correct?"

"Yeah, that's correct," answered the man.

"Are you Roy Warren Osborn?" the sergeant asked, looking at the suspects driver's license.

"I am. Are you done here? I want to leave."

"Not so fast," said the sergeant. "Your driver's license expired more than two years ago. Why haven't you renewed it?"

The man being questioned did not respond, but simply stared at the sergeant.

"Sir, please step back away from the car."

The sergeant reached into the vehicle and removed the registration card from the steering column. He read the card and asked the man, "Is your girlfriend Norma Widick?"

The man did not answer.

"Sir, the registration card states that the vehicle belongs to Norma Widick who resides in Alhambra, California. You just told me that your girlfriend lives here in Las Vegas."

Then Schenkenberger stepped to the back door of the Chevy. He put on a pair of gloves out of caution not to taint anything he deemed might be evidence in an auto theft, such as fingerprints. He pulled out the duffle bag, and the crumpled shirt, and placed them on the hood of the car. He asked, "Is this your shirt?

The man shrugged his shoulders, but did not say a thing.

Is this your gun?" The sergeant gestured toward the gun in the duffle bag.

The man did not answer, but continued staring at the sergeant, then looked back over his shoulder at the other two officers.

"Mr. Roy Osborn, I am placing you under arrest." The sergeant nodded to the two officers to handcuff the suspect and place him under arrest.

"What in the hell for?" yelled Osborn as he tried to free himself from the grip of the officer putting handcuffs on him.

"For starters: auto theft. The registration on this vehicle says it belongs to a person in Alhambra, California, not Las Vegas, Nevada. We are going to want to talk to your girlfriend as soon as you give us her name and address to verify ownership of the vehicle," said the sergeant. "We are going to impound the car to examine the broken window and the stains that are noticeable throughout the vehicle. Any, and all, items in the vehicle will remain in police custody until further notice."

"This is bullshit! Ya don't have any right to arrest me," yelled Osborn.

His protest went ignored. The officer performed the standard operating practice: cuffed him and placed him in the back seat of the patrol car.

Schenkenberger spoke to the two officers, "When you get back to the station, fingerprint Mr. Osborn. My suspicion, right now, is that the car is stolen. We need to determine how he came in possession of the vehicle. He will appear before the judge, or justice of the peace, first thing Monday morning. If he is released from custody before we find the vehicle owner, he will likely flee the area, and we won't see him again."

The officers transported him to the LVPD police station. They booked him into the LVPD holding cell just past 3:00 a.m.

Sergeant Schenkenberger filled out the necessary paperwork outlining the nature and cause of the arrest. He walked into the shift captain's office to debrief him on the events that just transpired.

He told the captain, "There is something bothering me about this suspect. The car, the gun, the broken window, I think there is more to this than just a stolen vehicle. I don't want to see him cut loose from custody before we know what actually happened. I am sure he will flee the area and we will have a difficult time solving the car issue."

The captain said, "I will have a courier take your report to the on-call clerk at the courthouse to schedule an initial appearance for the suspect and the Justice of the Peace (JP) on Monday. Beyond that our hands are tied. You will have to get the information you need within the next 48 hours or the JP will likely let him go on minimum bail.

"The courts are normally open Monday through Friday from 8:00 a.m. to 5:00 p.m. You know as well as I do, crime does not keep those hours. Nevada law allows for the suspect to be detained for a maximum of 72 hours if a felony is believed to have been committed. Grand theft auto, which is why you arrested him, is a felony in Nevada. Detaining the suspect any longer than that can violate his rights to a speedy trial by state statute. By Monday, the District Attorney, and the JP, will have reviewed the auto theft charges. The JP will explain the charges to the suspect, ask him if he understands them, and ask if he needs a court appointed attorney to represent him, or if he wants to hire his own attorney. The JP will also determine if bail should be set, and at what amount."

Schenkenberger interrupted the captain and said, "Can we recommend to the DA that bail be set as high as the courts will allow. I don't want the suspect to be able to make bail. The man we arrested has no family, or ties, to the Las Vegas area. Releasing him on bail would more than likely assure that he would run, leave the state, and there would probably be no accountability to the auto theft."

"The best we can do at this time is forward our recommendation to the DA. I would like to hear from the vehicle owner. That would shed some light on the damage to the car, possible blood stains and why the suspect claimed possession of it," said the captain. "See if you can raise someone at the address on the registration. It's not likely. They are probably visiting here in Vegas and may not even know their car is missing yet. You have until Monday morning, good luck."

Photo source: Gary Mauri
1957 Chevy 4-door Sedan
Exact make and model of Norma's car

CHAPTER FOURTEEN

Shocking Discovery

At approximately 6:00 a.m., the LVPD received a call from a private small craft airport. They said that a pilot in the vicinity of Blue Diamond Road, east of Las Vegas Boulevard, radioed in to the tower that there may be two bodies on the road. The pilot identified himself as an employee of the nearby Atomic Energy Commission, Charlie Dickinson. Mr. Dickinson and a friend were searching the area from their small plane looking for a reported abandoned car near Blue Diamond Road. They intended to salvage the car for parts. The pilot told the air traffic controller that his passenger in the plane scoured the area using binoculars. He requested that the tower notify the LVPD. The pilot said he circled back over the area and confirmed that there were two bodies lying face down on the side of the asphalt road.

The LVPD immediately dispatched a patrol unit, and notified the County Sheriff's Office. The area described is in Clark County, and in the Las Vegas area of city impact. The LVPD and the LV Sheriffs' Office jointly patrolled the area.

At nearly the same time that the pilot notified the air traffic control tower, a Clark County resident, Bruce Cook, left for work at a nearby auto parts distribution warehouse. The sun, just rising above the horizon, yellow and amber colors lit up the desert surface in spectacular rays of light. He lived in the unincorporated area of Clark County, about 6 miles outside the city limits of Las Vegas. The population is sparse in this area. Bruce Cook's few neighbors were no less than a half-mile apart.

Bruce left his home and drove west along the two-lane Blue Diamond Road for about a mile until it intersected at Las Vegas Boulevard. Shortly after leaving his residence, and before he reached Las Vegas Boulevard, Bruce noticed something off to his left that did not appear normal. He began to slow down his car as he drove past some objects on the desert floor next to the roadway.

He stopped his vehicle and backed it up. The sun just above the horizon, brought a mixture of light and shadows that he thought were playing tricks on him. He parked his car on the opposite side of the road, he stepped out of his vehicle and approached the objects laying on the desert floor. As he approached, he suddenly froze. There were two bodies lying on the road, two obviously dead bodies. He approached close enough to identify the bodies as females. He noticed tire tracks in the sand at the same location. Standing still, observing the scene, he noticed two pocketbooks. The contents of the pocketbooks were strewn about 100 feet from where the bodies were lying. Trying to shake off the shock of what he saw, he turned and went back to his vehicle. He noticed a low flying plane circling the area, but did not waste any time to try and figure out what the pilot might be doing. Hurriedly turning his vehicle around, he drove back to his residence, and called the Clark County Sheriff's office.

The sheriff's dispatcher took the information, and thanked Mr. Cook for reporting what he saw alongside the road. She also appreciated him giving them an accurate location. An officer would be dispatched immediately. The dispatcher asked Mr. Cook if he would wait near the scene but not to go near the bodies. He said he would. Then Bruce Cook notified his workplace. He told them he might be late this morning, and gave a brief description of what he found about a mile from his house.

The County Sheriff's Deputy, and an LVPD officer, arrived at the location at nearly the same time; about 15 minutes after they received the reporting call. They quickly cordoned off the area and requested assistance from the county Medical Examiner, and the forensic team. Sheriff Deputy Rick Carione, confirmed the two victims were female, but he could not tell how long ago they were dumped on the side of the road. The Deputy observed two purses and their contents strewn about the area near the bodies. Driver's licenses identified the two women as Inez Malloy from San Gabriel, California, and Norma Widick from Alhambra, California.

The LVPD officer recognized the names from a report that he read when he came on his shift the night before. He remembered reading a report about an abandoned vehicle, a pick-up truck, found in a hotel parking lot. The vehicle belonged to a person reportedly missing; Gaynard Widick. Gaynard's wife, Norma, and his mother-in-law, Inez Malloy, and Gaynard's parents picked up the truck yesterday afternoon at the LVPD impound yard. The report, filed by Detective H. Frieler, also noted that officers were to 'stop and detain' Mr. Gaynard Widick. The LVPD officer, Joe Flinn, talked to the county deputy and told him that there may be a possible connection to this crime scene and a pick-up truck found at a Las Vegas hotel parking lot.

Officer Flinn said, "I am going to have dispatch see if they can contact Detective Frieler and have him come out here. For the time being, this should be handled as an LVPD case until we can sort it all out. One of our detectives met these two women just yesterday afternoon."

"That's fine by me," said Deputy Carione. "Less paper work for me. The investigators, and M.E., will stay on site and assist you on the evidence gathering and help document their findings."

Officer Flinn radioed back to the station. He asked the dispatcher to contact Detective Frieler at his residence and ask him if he can drive to the scene on Blue Diamond Road.

Detective Frieler woke to the ring of the phone. His wife picked it up. The dispatcher identified herself and asked to speak to the detective.

The dispatcher said, "Detective, I just received a request from officer Flinn that you respond to a scene where two bodies were discovered. The officer requested your presence at a probable homicide location just east of Las Vegas Boulevard on Blue Diamond Road. The preliminary identification of the victims makes them out to be Inez Malloy and Norma Widick. Officer Flinn is asking for you because he read in his briefing report that you met with the two women just yesterday afternoon."

"I did meet them yesterday. Please let Officer Flinn know that I will be there as quickly as possible," the detective said.

The detective felt a bit of anger and a bit of sadness at the same time. *Two pleasant women were trying to make sense of a missing husband and an abandoned vehicle, and now someone has murdered them!*

CHAPTER FIFTEEN

A Desert Crime Scene

When Frieler arrived on the scene, the sun had already risen well above the horizon. The air still felt cool, but the detective knew it would be warming up quickly in the desert sun. Outside of town, the desert seemed quiet and peaceful. Studying the scene, the detective thought the desert belied anything but quiet and peaceful for the two victims. He observed a lot of activity: six police cars, an ambulance, and the van from the Las Vegas County Medical Examiner's office, and a couple of vehicles from the county and LVPD forensic divisions.

Officer Flinn said, "My apologies for waking you up so early. I requested that you be contacted because I read your report about the abandoned vehicle, the pick-up truck, that you turned over to the two victims yesterday afternoon. The two victims appear to be Norma Widick, and her mother, Inez Malloy. This will evolve from an abandoned vehicle to a homicide case. The LVPD Robbery and Homicide Division will get the assignment. More than likely, it will be your case because of your initial involvement. I informed the deputy that the LVPD Robbery and Homicide Division, will likely be the lead investigators in this crime. I thought you would want to see the death scene before we remove everything."

"You are probably right, this will more than likely be an LVPD case. I want to keep the sheriff's office involved. By all appearances, we have a double homicide on our hands. The county M.E., forensic team and their crime lab will be very useful in helping to solve this. Walk me through what you have discovered to this point," said Detective Frieler.

The officer said, "It appears that both women were shot in the head and dumped here along the road. The M.E. estimates the time of death between midnight and 2:00 a.m. this morning. It appears both were killed at the scene, most likely in a vehicle. The patrol division has located what they believe to be Mrs. Widick's' vehicle near a hotel parking lot.

"They may have gotten a break about three or four hours ago. A sergeant and two officers detained an adult male trying to reclaim the vehicle. They found a gun in the back seat, a shattered side window, and what may be blood stains on the seat. Right now, there is no solid connection between the suspect and these two women. The only connection is that he attempted to claim custody of the vehicle. He told the officer that the car belonged to his girlfriend. He would not give the name of his girlfriend to the officers, but told them she lives in Las Vegas. The vehicle is registered in California to one of the victims."

"The suspect is being held at the downtown station?" asked the detective.

"Yes, arrested and booked on suspicion of auto theft because his story did not add up for the responding officers," said Flinn.

"Anything else you can tell me?" asked the detective.

"We found the contents of their purses scattered about the crime scene. The identification information leads us to believe these victims are the ones that belong to the contents we found." Flinn gestured with his hands in a sweeping motion over the area. "We did not find any money, so it also appears that the suspect went through the purses looking for cash and took whatever he found."

Officer Flinn rubbed his chin and glanced over to where the two bodies were covered with sheets. "I hope you find whoever did this."

"We will," said the detective, "Let me know if you find anything else. I am going to head into the station and see if I can get the suspect to talk to me."

"One more thing," Flinn added, "I want you to take a look at something we found on the bodies."

The officers and Detective Frieler walked over to where the forensic team placed white sheets over each of the bodies. Carefully stepping so he would not disturb the immediate area around the bodies where the forensic team placed identifying markers in the painstaking process of taking photos of the crime scene. Officer Flinn pulled one of the sheets away from the body, which he said appeared to be Mrs. Malloy. "It is bad enough that they were shot execution style—a bullet to the head. But look at this. The M.E. believes that both women were also *run over* by the vehicle after they were shot." The officer pointed out tire tracks that were visible on their clothing.

The detective shook his head in disbelief and disgust at the callousness of the crime. "You will probably be here for a while. The information from the forensic team will help us re-create what transpired at this location. The M.E. will examine the bodies more thoroughly once he gets them back to the morgue. I'll follow up on his reports. The M.E. will also determine if the victims were raped. Murder, robbery, theft, rape: the charges against the perpetrator are mounting up rather fast. I hope we catch this person real soon.

"It won't take the newspapers long to learn about this, and I'll have to locate the next of kin to inform them before they read about it or hear it on the evening news. Do your best to keep the media away from the scene."

"You got it," said the officer. "I'll be in touch as soon as we are finished here."

The detective returned to his late model, unmarked, vehicle and drove into headquarters to begin the interrogation of the suspect. He did not want to make any assumptions that there might be a connection between the stolen vehicle and the murders. Those details would reveal themselves soon enough. Detective Frieler could not have imagined that the interrogation of the man being detained would create more suspicion and more questions connected to this heinous crime.

CHAPTER SIXTEEN

The Interrogation

Shortly after the arrest of Roy Warren Osborn, the LVPD Watch Commander, Randy Schuh, looked over the identification of suspect Osborn and noticed the Oregon Driver's License showed a Portland address. He followed up by contacting the Portland PD to find out if there were any wants or warrants on Mr. Oswald. He also requested any criminal background records on the man they were detaining. Schuh learned the individual in custody amassed an extensive criminal record that included petty theft, burglary, grand theft, and armed robbery. The latter led to a 5-year prison sentence. Roy Warren Osborn, whose birth date on his driver's license says he is 36 years old, bounced in and out of trouble with the law since the age of eleven.

Detective Frieler met one of his fellow detectives, Paul Cooper, before meeting the suspect. He requested that Detective Cooper accompany him in this initial meeting on the auto theft charge. Cooper logged more than eight years' experience in the Robbery and Homicide Division. Frieler and Cooper worked on other cases that required both detectives to interrogate suspected criminals. The two worked well together. He briefly went over the circumstances involving the arrest and his suspicion of the suspect being connected to the homicides.

Frieler told Cooper, "I'm not one hundred percent sure if the suspect in custody is the same one that committed the homicides. I expect that fact to become a lot clearer once we open up the discussion on the car theft. If you are ready, I'd like to get the conversation started."

"I'm ready, let's do this," said Cooper. The two of them stepped into the interrogation room at approximately 9:00 a.m.

Detective Frieler sat directly across from the suspect. Detective Cooper sat at the end of the table nearest to Frieler and the left side of the suspect. The LVPD kept the interrogation room void of furniture, except for a metal rectangular table and the three chairs.

"Mr. Osborn, do you know why you are being detained?" asked Frieler.

Osborn, no stranger to being asked questions by the police, acted as though sitting in a police station with two detectives did not make him nervous. The handcuffs arounds his wrists were secured to the top of the table. The LVPD used 12-inch chains attached to the handcuffs and table to restrict movement. That is a long-standing police protocol: minimize the suspects ability to attempt to overpower the detectives.

He appeared disheveled. His hair appeared to have not been combed in days and his blood shot eyes led the detectives to believe the suspect did not get much sleep. His face revealed that it may not have been close to a razor in the past 24 to 48 hours. That's understandable. A person in custody would not be given a razor upon entering the police holding cell. His bloodshot eyes would not hold eye contact with the detectives.

Both detectives, having been through this before, look for body language signs. Osborn, hands clasped together, placed and rested them on the table. The detective saw that his hands were perspiring, leaving tell-tale signs of perspiration on the metal table. He could not hide his anxiousness even though he tried not to show it.

"I went to get my girlfriend's car, and they arrested me on suspicion of auto theft. It's all bullshit!"

Osborn began to fidget. He moved forward in his chair, placing his elbows on the table. He stared directly at Detective Frieler, but broke eye contact and glanced around the room.

Detective Cooper said, "We want to clear up a few things unrelated to the auto theft, and thought you might want to talk to us, so we can clear you of any wrong doing. Are you OK with that?"

Osborn did not answer. Nor did he move, other than a slight, but noticeable rubbing together of his clasped hands.

Det. Cooper said, "Let's establish your place of residence. Your driver's license says that you live in Portland, Oregon. Is that Correct?"

"Yep," he replied.

The detective waited to see if Osborn would add more to his answer. He did not.

"How long have you been in Las Vegas?" The detective did not look at the suspect when he asked the question. He opened a manilla folder and shuffled through some papers waiting for Osborn to give an answer.

After a short pause, Osborn said, "I arrived several days ago."

"How did you get here?" Cooper asked, turning over a paper in his folder, then looking at Osborn, waiting for his answer.

"I hitched a ride," he said.

"You hitch hiked from Portland to Las Vegas?" Cooper asked.

"Yeah." Osborn slid back in the chair, sliding his hands and elbows off the table.

Det. Frieler asked, "What route did you take to get here? How many rides did you get along the route?"

"I took the 101 from Portland to Los Angeles. I got lucky and a trucker picked me up just outside of Portland that brought me all the way to L.A. He said he's heading southbound to San Diego. Then I got another ride just east of L.A. on the 15 that brought me here. The guy that picked me up said he's heading to Las Vegas."

Cooper asked, "What brought you to Las Vegas?"

"I wanted to check out the job situation," he said.

"You are unemployed?" Cooper asked.

"That's right," he said. "It's difficult to find work in Portland."

"We contacted the authorities in Portland, and they did not paint a very rosy picture of you. They informed us that you have a history of run-ins involving the law that spans the past two decades. The last, and most recent, encounter involved an armed robbery charge. You were convicted of that and spent 5 years in the Oregon penal system. Is that why it's hard to find work?" Frieler asked.

No response came from the suspect. He sat in his chair, arms now resting on his legs. He looked down at the floor, still making little to no eye contact.

"You said that you arrived in Las Vegas several days ago. How many days ago? Four days? A week? When did you get here?" Frieler asked.

"Last weekend," Osborn replied, his voice now noticeably more irritated.

"That would be seven days ago," the detective stated.

"Do you remember the names of the drivers that picked you up when you hitchhiked here?" asked Frieler.

"No."

"You said that a trucker brought you to Los Angeles. Did another trucker bring you to Las Vegas?"

"No. I got a ride in a pick-up truck to Las Vegas," he said.

"Tell us the make of the truck," said Frieler.

"I don't know," Osborn replied.

"You don't know? Ford, or a Chevy? Do you remember the color?"

"No. I did not pay any attention to the truck. I wanted a ride and I got one," said Osborn.

"What do you remember about the driver?" Cooper asked. "Big guy, a small guy? Did he have long hair, short hair, bald? Color of his hair?"

Increasingly irritated, Osborn said, "I don't know, and I couldn't care less what he looked like."

"Where did the drivers stop along the way? What did they stop for?"

Osborn took a deep breath and exhaled slowly. He looked directly at Cooper and said, "I don't know where they stopped. I might have been sleeping."

Cooper held eye contact with Osborn, then said, "Help me out here, Roy. Is it all right if I call you Roy?"

Osborn held the detectives gaze, but did not answer.

"I'm trying to understand something," said Cooper. "Did you have some business in L.A.? Maybe someone you were visiting? I can't understand why you would take that route to Las Vegas from Portland. It is not the shortest, most direct route."

Osborn broke his eye contact. He moved forward in his chair, putting his hands and arms back on the table. giving no answers, shaking his head as if to say you are wasting your time.

Frieler broke the short silence and said, "Last night, when you were detained and brought to the station, you refused to give the officers the name of your girlfriend, who you also told the officers is the owner of the car, is that correct?"

Osborn did not respond to the question but continued to shift his gaze from Frieler to Cooper.

"Mr. Osborn," said Frieler, "It is important for us, and more important for you, that we clear up the ownership of the vehicle. If you want to be cleared of the auto theft charge, we need to talk to your girlfriend who you said owns the car."

A noticeable long pause filled the interview room. Osborn did not reply. The detectives waited for him to say something, and make an effort to possibly clear himself. Osborn did not break the long silence. He slid back into his chair and sat quietly staring at one detective, and then the other.

"Mr. Osborn," Det. Frieler said, breaking the silence, "I hope you understand the dilemma we have here, or should I say, 'the predicament that you are in.' We don't believe that you have a girlfriend in Las Vegas that owns the vehicle you tried to claim in the early hours this morning.

"The vehicle appears to have blood stains on the seat, windows and dashboard area. The arresting officers said that you told them the duffle bag found in the back seat of the vehicle belonged to you. In that duffle bag they found a .38 caliber handgun. That would indicate you were in possession of a fire arm. It is illegal for a felon to be in possession of a firearm in Oregon or Nevada. The firearm found in the car, in your duffle bag, had two empty casings, and four live rounds—all of them still in the cylinder. Shortly after 6:00 a.m. this morning, we received a call that two bodies were found, gunshot wounds to the head on both victims. The bodies were left or dumped on the side of the road, about five miles outside of town. One of the victims, left on the side of the road, is the true registered owner of the vehicle. That person does not live in Las Vegas, or even Nevada. Now, right now, is the time for you to help yourself, and clear some of this up."

No response came from the suspect, he just sat in his chair. He did not make eye contact but seemed to focus directly at the collar on the detective's shirt. Frieler and Cooper allowed a longer than usual silence to continue in the interrogation room.

Finally, Frieler said, "Mr. Osborn, in addition to the auto theft charge, we are tacking on kidnapping, robbery, illegal possession of a firearm, and the murder of the two women we found on the roadway earlier this morning. I have asked the Medical Examiner to notify me once he completes his work at the county morgue. If he tells me the women were raped, those charges are going to be tacked on also."

"Bullshit, this is all bullshit! I want a lawyer! I did not murder anyone! I don't know anything about any murders!" Osborn screamed.

"Roy Warren Osborn, I'm sure you know that the laws in Nevada probably mirror the laws in Oregon, which I'm sure you're quite familiar. You will have your initial appearance before a justice of the peace on Monday. If you were making any plans to go anywhere soon, you might want to change your itinerary. I think you are going to be a guest of the State of Nevada for quite a while." Frieler said as he leaned forward in his chair closing the gap between himself and Osborn.

Detective Cooper stood, walked the short distance across the interrogation room and opened the door. Two uniformed officers stepped inside to escort Osborn back to his cell.

"You are wrong" He yelled at the detectives. "I did not kill anyone!"

Frieler said, "Officers, please escort Mr. Osborn to the Custody Suite."

"Custody Suite?" asked one of the officers.

"Yes, he's going to be staying in Las Vegas for a while. We will make his stay as comfortable and pleasant as possible. Tuck him in if necessary."

"Yes sir," said the officer as they escorted Osborn out of the interrogation room.

"Custody Suite," said Cooper laughing. "I haven't heard that one before."

Frieler smiled as they exited the interview room and walked through the corridor to the Robbery & Homicide offices. Frieler glanced over at Cooper and said, "Thoughts?"

Cooper replied, "There were a lot of silent alarms going off in that meeting. We might have another homicide on our hands, maybe we have a serial killer in custody. I could not help but notice fresh scratches on the left side of his cheek and on his forearm."

"I have the same concerns, and yes, I did notice the scratches. Can you have the photographer take some close-up shots of them," said Frieler. "I want to talk to the suspect again, but I want him to sit and think about what we just discussed. Let's follow up with Portland to find out if they have any pertinent information on this guy. We will need to explore every aspect of this homicide. If this Gaynard Widick is not another victim, could he have been involved? Did he lure his wife here?" Frieler shrugged his shoulders, giving thought to several possible scenarios involving Gaynard Widick.

"Cooper, give forensics a call to see what they have pieced together so far. It will probably take several days to do the ballistic testing, and blood analysis. I'll call the M.E. to find out if rape needs to be added to the suspects growing list of charges. I'm going to recommend to the captain that we request the FBI look over our shoulder at this crime. There may be another body out there between here and L.A. We might have an interstate crime suspect, or a possible serial killer, in custody. The FBI's network of information might turn up something else."

"You bet," said Cooper, "I'll stop in and see the captain and have him put out an urgent APB for Gaynard Widick. I'll contact the Alhambra PD, and LAPD, about our suspicion, so they are aware of another possible homicide."

"Hold off on contacting Alhambra and L.A. I'm not sure how I want to handle the notification of the next of kin for the two women. I might need help from Alhambra, or San Gabriel to do that, if we want to beat the press before the story gets printed, or hits the 5 o'clock news," said Frieler. "I'll take care of that right after I talk to the captain, so the other agencies get all the information at the same time. We have to find Gaynard Widick as soon as humanly possible. Let's start that ball rolling."

The LVPD issued a follow-up missing person's report that extended to the entire Western portion of the United States. Gaynard Widick's truck, found abandoned in Las Vegas, his wife picked it up yesterday afternoon, now she's dead. Gaynard allegedly stayed in Las Vegas for a few days, checked out of his hotel, and has not been seen, or heard from since. There were a lot of missing pieces to the homicide, and the detectives began reviewing evidence and facts, as they prepared for the upcoming initial court appearance on Monday.

Frieler contacted the Golden Nugget Hotel and Casino where Gaynard Widick reportedly stayed. He asked to speak to the hotel staff that checked Widick into the hotel and he wanted to talk to the hotel housekeeping personnel that cleaned the room. The hotel staff could not offer much help in answering the questions he asked. They did not know if he saw any visitors or how he spent his time at the hotel.

Detective Frieler contacted the L.V. District Attorney, Howard Gould. Being Sunday, he needed to rouse the DA at his residence prior to the initial appearance scheduled the following day. The DA listened to the report and expressed concern that if bail is set, and the suspect can make bail, he would undoubtedly flee the state. He requested all the reports from the officer on scene, the M.E. and the Forensics be sent to him along with information on the suspect. The LVPD, and the Clark County Prosecutors Office, intended to provide the information that would allow the justice of the peace to determine that a crime had been committed and that the suspect in custody is guilty of committing those crimes.

CHAPTER SEVENTEEN

Sucker Punch

T he LVPD knew that the local media would be reporting on the homicides as soon as they learned of the callous and horrific crimes. The detective needed to notify the next of kin as soon as possible. Logistically, the distance between Las Vegas and Los Angeles is too far for the LVPD to travel and notify the victims' relatives in person. Detective Frieler contacted the San Gabriel Police Department and spoke to one of their detectives. He relayed the tragic incident and requested that the San Gabriel P.D. do a courtesy call to the Malloy residence, breaking the bad news, and asking that the family contact Frieler at the LVPD for further information. As soon as contact could be made, Frieler would ask that the victims' family send someone to make positive identification of the women's bodies.

The San Gabriel Police Department dispatched two officers, Sergeant Frandsen and Officer Tate, to Tom Malloy's house. One of the most unpleasant duties of a police officer is notifying a family of the loss of their loved one. The police car pulled into the driveway leading to Tom's house. The policed officers noticed that the blinds were all pulled and closed on the windows. Frandsen said, "I wonder if anyone is home, it doesn't appear that there is.

Although, I see a car parked behind the house. Perhaps word of the homicides arrived here before we did."

They knocked on the door. Within a few short moments, Tom Malloy answered the knock on that Saturday morning.

One of the officers introduced himself to Tom as Sergeant Frandsen and the other officer as Officer Tate.

The sergeant asked, "Are you Mr. Malloy, Mr. Tom Malloy?"

"Yes, I am."

"Mr. Malloy," the sergeant said, "We have been dispatched by the San Gabriel Police Department to your residence, may we come in to talk to you?"

Tom peered at both officers, still a little surprised as to why they were at his house. He hesitated, then invited them to enter. The three men walked into the kitchen area and sat down at the table. Tom asked them why they were at his house.

"Mr. Malloy, we are sorry to inform you that your wife and daughter were shot and killed earlier this morning just outside of Las Vegas, Nevada."

Tom Malloy felt as though he had been hit by a sucker punch. He did not expect this, his mind would not believe what his ears were hearing. Painful, and debilitating, he tried to gather his senses from what he heard, but he believed the impact to be too great. He did not know if he could recover from this unbelievable news, or if he wanted to. The pain felt more mental than physical. He felt his entire body succumbing to a numbness. This feeling, foreign to him, left him unable to understand the meaning of what he just heard; the worst possible news of his life.

Tom did not move from the chair at the kitchen table, he just stared at the two officers. Incapable of talking or moving, he felt completely helpless. The officers could see the pain in Tom's eyes and the expression on his face spoke volumes about the pain in his mind. The sergeant's words delivered a blow that Tom believed stole him of his will to live. His wife of 32 years, and his youngest daughter; only 22 years old, somehow taken from him forever.

He could not organize any thoughts in his head. The blood rushed through his brain, he could not feel his legs, and could not command them to help him out of the chair. He sat still and mumbled the words, "My wife and my daughter were murdered? What do you mean by that? "How could this happen?"

One of the officers noticed that Tom looked like he might fall out of his chair. He reached out, took Tom by the elbow so he would remain upright.

Tom did not respond. He looked blankly past the officers.

The sergeant said, "Mr. Malloy, we do not have all the details of the tragedy. The crime occurred in Las Vegas very early this morning. The LVPD asked if we could notify the next of kin ASAP. We have a contact person in Las Vegas, Detective Harold Frieler, for you to call. He told one of our detectives that he would make himself available to talk to you anytime to answer questions. He would like to know if you or another relative can make arrangements to travel to Las Vegas to identify the bodies."

Tom could still not respond; he sat at the table in shock. This could not be happening—it is not possible that his wife and daughter could have been murdered.

His eyes glistening, he said, "This is not making sense to me. I just talked to my wife, and daughter, I hugged them, I kissed them goodbye just yesterday. They were going to return home today. I don't understand." Barely audible Tom murmured, "This is not right, it's not normal, parents aren't supposed to outlive their children. This can't be true."

The weight of the pain kept him in the chair. He made no effort to get up, and he could not communicate very well when the police asked questions.

Sergeant Frandsen asked, "Is there someone we can call that can come over and help you?"

Tom looked up at the sergeant and said, "Call my daughter, Margie, she lives in Glendora." He nodded in the direction of the phone. Next to the phone sat a personal phone book that contained her number.

The officer located her number in the book under M and dialed it on the black rotary dial phone. No one answered even after almost 20 rings.

The police officer looked at Tom and said, "I'm sorry, no one is answering the phone. We can call the Glendora P.D. and ask them to send a unit to the residence if you would like."

Tom nodded, and mumbled, "Yes, thank you." He continued to stare, still struggling, trying to understand the debilitating message that the two police officers brought to his door.

The sergeant, not wanting to leave Tom on his own, asked, "Is there another family member that we can contact for you?"

Tom said, "I have a son. But I do not know where he is. I don't have a number that works anymore. My wife has brothers and sisters in the area. I don't want them to hear about this from the police. I need Margie's help to do that."

The sergeant nodded and then contacted headquarters to inform them of the situation, including Tom Malloy's shock at hearing the bad news. The sergeant requested that the dispatcher contact the Glendora P.D. to send a courtesy car to Mrs. Mauri's home. He gave them the address and phone number. He said they would stand by a little while longer until the Glendora P.D. tried to make contact with Tom's other daughter.

CHAPTER EIGHTEEN

Unbelievable

Approximately 1:30 p.m. in the afternoon, Margie and Jimmy Mauri and their three children returned from a picnic at a nearby park. A fun filled day that would take a turn for the worse. The kids were still burning off some energy running around in the front yard when a patrol car pulled up in front of their house within minutes after the Mauri's arrived home. Their son, Gary, heard the phone ringing in the house and ran to answer it.

The caller identified herself as the dispatcher from the Glendora P.D. Jimmy walked in the house behind his son. Gary shrugged and handed the phone to his dad.

Margie and their two daughters, Beth Ann, and Lisa, were gathering up the blankets and picnic supplies out of the car. They girls were talking excitedly about a large pine cone they found in the park.

An officer got out of the car and started walking toward Margie. She thought this to be highly unusual—police officers did not make house calls unless they were needed for assistance. Margie, feeling both surprise and suspicion, watched as the officer approached her.

Before the officer could say anything, Margie asked, "Can I help you?"

He identified himself as Officer Scott Davis and asked, "Are you Margie Mauri?"

"Yes, I am. What is this about?"

Over her shoulder, she could hear her husband talking on the phone. She heard him say that Margie is talking to a police officer at the moment. Jimmy hung up the phone after saying goodbye. He went outside to where Margie and the officer were standing. Gary followed him.

The officer said, "We were sent here at the request of the Alhambra Police Department. Two of their officers are at your father's house and he has asked for you. They were not able to reach you by phone, and asked if we would do a courtesy call."

Margie's eyes grew large as she felt her heart beat quicken. Fearing that something awful happened to her dad she said, "What is it? Did he get hurt, was he in an accident? Is he in the hospital?"

The officer said, "Margie, your dad is okay. There has been an incident involving your mother and sister in Las Vegas. Your dad would like for you to come to his house in San Gabriel right away."

"What kind of incident?" Margie asked while holding direct eye contact with the officer.

"I do not have much information. My partner and I were in the area, and received a radio call to check, and see, if Margie Mauri is home, and to relay the request to contact her father as soon as possible."

Her mind raced as she thought of what could have happened to her mother and sister. Her heart began to beat faster as she felt it more difficult to breathe. She struggled to collect her thoughts.

Margie managed to say, "Thank you and excuse me," to the officer, and hurried into the house to call her dad.

Her anxiety grew when Sergeant Frandsen answered the phone. She asked, "Is my dad okay?"

The sergeant said, "Yes, he would like to talk to you," and handed the phone to Tom.

Tom took the phone, "Margie," he said slowly, "something awful has happened. Can you come over here right away?"

"Dad, what is it?"

"I don't know what to make of this." Tom's voice cracked, and he struggled to break the horrible news to his daughter. Then he said, "The police are here and said that your mother and sister have been murdered in Las Vegas. Can you come over now, please?"

The phone fell out of Margie's hand. She felt a weakness consume her as tears rolled down her cheeks.

Jimmy reached for Margie's arm then bent down and picked up the phone. He said; "Tom, this is Jimmy—what is going on?"

Jimmy listened in silence, tears filled his eyes. He asked sullenly, "How is this possible? Are you sure? We are driving over right now. We'll be there as soon as possible."

Margie could not hide her trembling, fear, shock, and sadness from her children. She looked at them and saw that they were scared. Her kids were not used to seeing their mother cry. Now they were seeing tears in the eyes of both their parents. Margie could not stop her tears. She knelt down in front of the kids.

"Something has happened to Grandma, and Aunt Norma. Your dad and I need to go to Grandpa's house right away." She looked at her three young children, grabbed them to her as she cried. Her children began crying, too. Margie hugged them tighter. *They will never see their grandma, or Aunt Norma again.*

Fighting back her tears, she looked at her husband and said, "Will you call Jackie next door to watch the kids? We should go soon, but I don't think I can drive."

Jimmy Mauri went next door to the neighbor's house and asked if she could watch the kids for a few hours as he and Margie needed to respond to an emergency right away at her dad's house in San Gabriel. Margie hurriedly packed some clothes as she expected to stay overnight at her dad's house. Jimmy could return home and take care of the kids and anything else that needed attention.

By the time they reached San Gabriel, Margie felt a bit more composed, or so she thought.

The police left her parent's house before she and Jimmy arrived. When she walked into the house, her emotions overwhelmed her. A flood of thoughts and unanswered questions poured into her already frail state of mind. She did not say anything, too overwhelmed by grief when she saw her dad. Tears streamed down her face. She hugged her dad and then slipped away from him, and collapsed onto the couch.

When her tears slowed, Margie sat up and asked her dad, "How could this happen? Has anyone heard from Gaynard?"

Tom shook his head and said, "There has not been any word, or news, about Gaynard. No one seems to know where the hell he is. Margie, the LVPD needs to have someone from the family go to Las Vegas to make a positive identification of your mother and sister. Would you be up for that? We need to make arrangements to bring them home. I have a number for Detective Frieler in Las Vegas."

Jimmy answered, "We can do that. Margie and I will go to Las Vegas and make arrangements to bring Inez and Norma home. If we cannot get out of here by tomorrow, we will go first thing Monday morning."

Margie looked at him and mumbled, "Thank you. I want to go back home this afternoon and see the kids again before we leave for Las Vegas. I could tell that my emotional state earlier today before we left scared them and made them cry." Like her dad, she could not understand what happened, how could they have been murdered? What set this tragedy in motion? She knew she needed to focus on her mother and sister by going to Vegas to take care of things and get some answers. *There is so much to do, and I don't know where to start. I just want my mom and my sister.*

Margie asked her dad, "Have you heard from Mitchell?"

"No. None of the phone numbers that I have work. There is no way to tell him what has happened, I have no idea where he is."

"We need to call Inez's brothers, sisters and her dad to let them know what happened. I just can't seem to gather my thoughts long enough to do that," Tom added.

Jimmy said, "I'll do that, Tom. Why don't you and Margie discuss the funeral arrangements. I'll call the San Gabriel Mission also, and let them know that we will need to talk to the priest that will preside over the services. We probably cannot set a date, until we've heard from the LVPD and the Medical Examiner."

Jimmy sat down by the phone and began contacting Inez's birth family. He phoned her brother, Chuck, first. Chuck's wife, Eleanor, answered.

Jimmy said, "Hello Eleanor, this is Jimmy Mauri, is Chuck there? I need to talk to him."

"He is not," she said. "He is over at Louie's. They're working on a utility truck that Louie bought. Is there anything I can help you with?"

"I wish there could be, Eleanor. I have some very bad news. I'm calling all of Inez's family. Inez and Norma were murdered last night, or early this morning in Las Vegas. They went there to pick up Gaynard's abandoned truck. His parents went also and drove the truck home yesterday. Inez and Norma were going to spend the night, but encountered some car trouble."

"Oh no!" said Eleanor, "Chuck is going to be devastated. Do you want me to call him?"

"I probably should do that," said Jimmy. "Margie and I are here at Tom's right now. If any of them want to talk to Tom, this would be a good time." They said goodbye and Jimmy called Louie's house.

Frieda, Louie's wife, answered the phone.

Jimmy said, "I just got off the phone with Eleanor, and she said that Chuck and Louie were both there working on a truck, could you get both of them for me, I really need to talk to them."

Frieda went outside and said, "Jimmy Mauri is on the phone. He said he needs to talk to both of you, and it seems urgent."

Chuck and Louie took a moment to clean the grease off their hands, then both of them hurried into the house. Frieda went back to the phone to let Jimmy know they would be in as soon as they cleaned up a bit. The two brothers entered the house, immediately sensing that something is wrong. Frieda's eyes were tearing as she looked at Louie and held out the phone. She said, "It's Jimmy, he has some very bad news."

Jimmy told Inez's brothers that their sister and niece were murdered in Las Vegas and that he and Margie would be going there to identify them and hopefully get some answers."

Both men were shocked to near disbelief that their sister, and niece, were killed. "Jimmy," Louie said, "I'll call Buster and our dad." Buster is the nickname given to their older brother, William. Buster and Inez's dad were both residing in Fort Dodge, Iowa.

Next, Jimmy called Inez's sister, Dorothy (Eastwood) Ponsness.

She and her family settled in North Idaho in the small community of Rathdrum. The Ponsness family enjoyed the vast fishing and hunting opportunities in North Idaho. Her husband, Lloyd, invented one of the first shotgun reloading machines.

Dorothy's youngest son, Stan, answered the phone. Jimmy identified himself to Stan and asked to speak to his mother. Dorothy met Jimmy only a few times. The expression on her face revealed her surprise that he would be calling. When he explained why he called, Dorothy felt faint, her legs gave out and she collapsed. Stan, and his older brother, Denny, heard the commotion and ran to where their mother fell on the floor. They helped her up, and she asked if they would hand her the phone. Jimmy remained on the line.

Jimmy said, "I'm sorry to have to call you and deliver such bad news. I just talked to Chuck and Louie, and they too, are shocked by what has happened. All of us are shocked. It is just so unbelievable."

Dorothy asked, "Has a date been set for the funeral services?"

"Not yet," said Jimmy. "Margie and I have to go to Las Vegas and make arrangements to bring them home. We thought it necessary to contact the family before someone heard it on the news. We should know something early next week about the date for the funeral."

"How is Tom taking this?" asked Dorothy.

"Not very well."

"This is so sad," said Dorothy. "Lloyd is at the manufacturing shop; I will tell him what has happened. Let me know as soon as a date has been set for the funeral, and we will travel down to California."

Jimmy felt the weight of being the deliverer of such bad news. He could feel the pain and sorrow in each of Inez's siblings. He continued the calls and dialed Vera and Helen next. Vera, the oldest sister, and Helen, the youngest of the girls, were overwhelmed with sorrow. They asked Jimmy to call them as soon as a date could be set for the funeral and if there might be anything they could do to help. Both sisters said they would go to see Tom tomorrow and would bring over some food.

Jimmy looked at his watch. He spent over two hours making calls to deliver the bad news to Inez's siblings. He sat and stared at the phone after the last call. He thought about the reactions from each of her three sisters and three brothers. Inez is the aunt of 19 nieces and nephews, and six great-nieces and great-nephews. She served as the godmother to some of them. Inez, her husband, raised three children of her own, who gave her three grandchildren. He thought about how very much she will be missed.

Jimmy, feeling more depressed after each phone call, dialed the parish at the San Gabriel Mission, Tom and Inez's home church. After explaining why he called, the receptionist immediately put Father Brown on the phone. The priest knew Tom and Inez as long-time members of the church, and the service that they provided through their dry-cleaning business for the parish. Tom also served as an usher on Sunday mornings. The priest told Jimmy that he wanted to be there for Tom, and would leave now to visit him.

Jimmy appreciated the offer and knew this would help Tom in his most troubled time.

Meanwhile, after hearing the devastating news from Jimmy, the two brothers and Frieda sat down at the kitchen table to talk. Frieda reheated the coffee she made earlier that day and poured a cup for each of them. They sat silently for a few moments, adding sugar and cream to their coffee cup and stirring it a bit.

Then Chuck said, "This is a hell of a thing."

Louie, more solemn, said, "Yes, it is. I spoke to Inez a few weeks ago. She seemed a little perturbed with me when I asked her what in the hell has Mitchell been up to. I told her we haven't seen him in quite a while, and I told her I planned to track him down and find out what he's up to. She said it would probably make matters worse for me to try and contact him. Basically, she told me to let her and Tom handle it. I took that to mean for me to mind my own business."

"I have wondered about Mitchell myself," said Chuck. "He's a troubled kid, even though he is no longer a kid. Inez told me a month or so ago that she is afraid he is using drugs and may be working at a porn shop in L.A. Tom pushed him pretty hard to step into the family business.

"She also told me that Tom has shown signs of becoming increasingly paranoid. He always wants the blinds on the windows closed, so no one can see in the house. He suspects someone is always watching him, possibly someone from the government."

Frieda said, "We do not know a lot about Tom's family history. But it seems to me, his dad became ill just before Tom and Inez were married. I wonder if this is a hereditary condition: early Alzheimer's or schizophrenia."

"I asked one of the doctors in the psych ward at the hospital about that. The doc said it sounded like a form of paranoia if Tom believes someone is watching him. Depending on the severity of the condition, treatment can be recommended. Sometimes that requires a person to self-commit to the hospital, and they could be there for a while. Inez told me Tom would not have anything to do with that and she did not want to bring it up to him. She said he seems fine whenever they go out or go visiting, and it has not bothered him at work, that she knows of. He's not forgetful and seems to carry on a conversation as if nothing were wrong. But the thought that someone is outside trying to look into their house has become all too common." Chuck paused, took a sip of his coffee.

"It's not a good feeling to get news like this. Our last conversation seemed bothersome to her." said Louie.

"I hear you," said Chuck. "She's been distraught over Mitchell and not sure how to handle it. Give him some room and hope for the best is about all they can do. And, then she has Tom to worry about. I hope these murders don't push him over the top."

The three of them sat silently for a few moments, staring at their coffee cup. Louie asked if there were any more of the chocolate chip cookies left over from the other day.

Then Chuck said, "Margie and Jimmy are going to have their hands full for a while. I'm going to call Jimmy when I get home and let him know I am going to Las Vegas with the two of them. I don't think either one of them should have to identify the bodies. A gunshot to the head is not something they should have to see."

"I can go if you think it's necessary," said Louie.

"It might be better if you wouldn't mind checking in on Tom to see if he needs anything? I can't imagine how he must feel right now," said Chuck.

"Sure, I'll get cleaned up. Frieda and I can drive over to see him this afternoon."

Chuck spoke to Jimmy when he returned home that afternoon to tell him he would be joining then on the trip to Vegas. The three of them left for Las Vegas Monday morning.

They made small talk for the first hour of the trip. Then Jimmy told Chuck how much he appreciated him for coming along.

Jimmy said, "From the time I started to date Margie, asked her to marry me, and all through our marriage, Inez seemed like a second mother, and a good friend to me. Norma might as well have been my kid sister, I loved them both very much. My memories are all about the good times, the laughter, the family gatherings, the things we would all do together. Inez made Halloween costumes for our kids. Both Inez and Norma were always doting on all three of our children.

"Margie and I talked about identifying the bodies and I need you to hear this from me Chuck. I want to cling to those memories for the rest of my life. I don't want to remember them lying in the morgue, lifeless, and have all those fond memories tainted by what has happened to them."

Chuck understood that and said, "Hell, I did not expect either one of you to go into the morgue. I think it would be best if I went in alone."

Chuck, a World War II Veteran, would be more prepared, if anyone could be prepared, for the shock and horror that they were going to encounter in Las Vegas.

A moment of silence fell over the travelers, then Margie said, "I have to go in there. I have to see them. I have to say good-bye."

"Suit yourself, but if you change your mind, that would be alright. You can say your good-byes at the funeral. I really don't think it is necessary for you to see them," said Chuck.

Then Chuck asked Margie, "What is going on with your old man?"

Margie said, "I don't know. I am worried about him. He is gradually becoming more suspicious that someone is watching him. The shades and blinds on all the windows have to be closed so no one can see in the house.

Maybe getting him a dog would help to draw him out. A dog needs to go on walks and they are very sociable pets." Then in a light laugh she said, "Norma would breeze into their house and immediately open all the blinds and shades. Dad would utter a protest but it would not do any good. She would just tell him that she did not want to hear it." Margie looked at Chuck and said, "I love my sister, she's such a force of energy, everyone loved her."

"I already miss her, I miss them both. What do you think will happen to your dad?"

"Without my mom there to help him, I suspect his condition will gradually become worse. I know he could not make this trip. I just hope he does not do something awful like hurt himself or someone else," said Margie.

"Inez told me that she has not seen any tendency for him to get violent," said Chuck.

"I have not seen that either. I have not seen it all my life. But the stress he is under now raises my level of concern. We aren't comfortable letting him watch the kids by himself. It's not that we think he would do something crazy, we worry that he won't be paying close enough attention to keep them safe," she said.

"Well, we're going to have to keep a closer eye on him for a while. He might just shut down and give up all together. Did you and your mother talk about the possibility of having him committed to a state hospital for treatment?" asked Chuck.

"She told me that you suggested it to her and that she did not think it would be necessary. Like I said, Dad has not shown any signs of being unable to cope with everyday reality, he just has this weird suspicion about being watched, and it seems to be isolated to when he's home."

Jimmy said, 'You're right though, we'll need to check on him more often to make sure things don't get worse."

"I will try to stop by his place at least once-a-week on my way home from work. What about your brother, do you anticipate he'll step up and help out?" asked Chuck.

"Mitchell? I would not count on it," said Margie.

"I didn't think so. I need to talk to Mitchell, and I better do that sooner rather than later. Whatever is going on with him has been going on for too long."

"Good luck doing that," said Margie. "I wish I could put my finger on whatever the problem is, but I don't have any idea. Mitchell seemed a lot happier when we lived in Iowa. He played on the high school basketball team and made lots of friends. Mom and dad went to most of his games . . . he seemed to excel at basketball and really enjoyed that game. But, no sports for him when we moved to California. Just a steady withdrawal from everyone. It seems like he's been that way for more than ten years now."

A mileage sign appeared: Las Vegas 10 Miles.

CHAPTER NINETEEN

Paths Crossed

The trio arrived in Las Vegas about 2:00 p.m. Margie left a message with the LVPD operator the day before to let the detective know they would arrive on Monday to identify her family, and make arrangements to have them transported back to San Gabriel.

Both detectives, Cooper and Frieler, working feverishly on the homicides, met them at the LVPD station. After brief introductions, they walked to one of the interview rooms so the detectives could bring them up to date on their investigation.

Detective Cooper began the conversation, "We booked the suspect early Saturday morning. His initial appearance before a justice of the peace occurred earlier today. The JP advised the suspect of his rights and the seriousness of the charges being brought against him. His charges, for now, include two counts of murder, kidnapping, robbery and auto theft. The JP explained the seriousness of the crimes and asked the suspect if he understood what he is being told. Then the JP asked the suspect how he wanted to plea to the charges; guilty or not guilty. He pleaded not guilty. This came as no surprise. Most criminals plead not guilty.

"The suspect, when asked if he could afford an attorney, or if he needed to have one appointed by the court, replied that he wanted to represent himself. The JP explained that the Sixth Amendment allowed for a defendant to represent oneself. The court terminology for self-representation is 'Pro Se.' The JP also explained the risk of any individual attempting to defend themself in a criminal trial. Nonetheless, the accused insisted on defending himself. The JP told him he will assign a defense attorney as 'stand-by' advisory counsel. That will assure, to some degree, that the defendant's rights are not trampled on in the court room.

"The case will now go to District Court for a preliminary hearing. That date has yet to be set, but I expect it to occur within three or four weeks. The JP decided there would be no bail due to the double homicide charges. The auto theft, kidnapping and robbery charges add to the seriousness of the crimes. We are pleased with the decision that bail will not be granted. The suspect has no ties to the area or to the state. He is considered to be a very high-risk flight individual.

"He has been remanded to the Clark County Jail for now. We got a big break in the case when the suspect tried to reclaim the car that belonged to Norma. The arresting officers saved us a lot of trouble by detaining him. Otherwise, he would have certainly left the area, and we could be looking for him for quite a while."

"That's a lot of information," Margie said. "You said the suspect is pleading not guilty. If he did do it, do you have to prove he did, and can you prove it?"

Detective Frieler said, "He has denied any involvement in the murders since his arrest. The burden of proof will be in the hands of the state to demonstrate, without a doubt, that the defendant is guilty. We believe that will happen. The law says that everyone is innocent until proven guilty."

"How long does this usually last before there is a trial?" Jimmy asked.

"It could take anywhere from six months to a year. A plea of not guilty only triggers the preliminary hearing. There will be two of them; one for each of the murder victims. The preliminary hearing determines if the charges brought against the suspect should be heard before a jury of his peers—a full jury trial. Once we get past the preliminary hearings, and the judge confirms the murder information is sufficient to warrant a jury trial, he will send the case to a capital hearing. When that happens, the judge will set a trial date. That date can be 4 to 6 months after the prelim, and is sometimes based on the case load in the courts," said Detective Frieler.

Margie sighed and said, "We have to live with the uncertainty that this suspect did the crime until such time that a jury renders a decision? And that could be as long as another year?"

"Yes," said Frieler. "We are certain he did it. We just have to prove it, and we will. The FBI has also been contacted to verify the crime scene analysis, and to double check the ballistics, and blood samples in their labs. They have the undisputed best testing facilities in the country, if not the world. It is a common practice to involve the FBI whenever there is a multi-state capital crime. In this case, the suspect traveled from Oregon. Your mother and sister traveled from California, and the crime occurred in Nevada."

"Did my mother and sister suffer?" Margie asked.

Frieler glanced at Cooper, then back at Margie. "The Medical Examiner notified me a little over an hour ago with his preliminary report. He said that your mother had some severe internal contusions on her head. The M.E. also said that your sister was raped and he found bruises on her arms and legs. The Clark County DA is also adding that charge to the crimes. Your sister most likely put up a struggle but to no avail. We do not have all the pieces yet as to what transpired. It appears that your mother might have been hit in the head several times. We suspect he used the butt of the gun and that may have rendered her unconscious. Then he shot them both in the back of the head from point blank range. They died instantly. What happened in the final 30 or 60 minutes of their lives we are not sure about. I'm sorry you had to hear that. We will recreate what we believed happened at the locksmith parking lot and up to the point where they were shot. The suspect is not cooperating by providing pertinent information. He clammed up, refusing to talk."

Margie felt distraught, and terrible, hearing what her mother and sister went through in those final horrifying minutes. Jimmy put his hand on hers. Chuck folded his arms across his chest and shook his head in disgust muttering a few expletives about the man in custody.

"I can't tell my dad what happened to Norma, it will kill him." Jimmy wrapped both arms around her and she leaned into him. She looked up at her husband and said, "He will have to hear this from us, won't he?"

Cooper spoke up and said, "We don't want to cause you any more grief and worry than what you are already experiencing, but we need to talk to you about Norma's husband, Gaynard Widick."

Margie looked at the detectives and did not say anything. She gestured with open hands, palms up, as if to say, *I don't know much about Gaynard.*

The detective slid a picture of a man across the table and asked, "Do you recognize this person?"

Jimmy, Margie and Chuck studied the photo. All three stated they did not recognize the person.

Detective Cooper said, "His name is Roy Warren Osborn. His driver's license tells us that he is a resident of Portland, Oregon. He claimed that the car, Norma's 1957 Chevy, belonged to his girlfriend. His story will be thoroughly vetted, and the LVPD will need to talk to other relatives and acquaintances of Norma and Inez. Is there any possibility that Norma knew the person in the photo?"

Margie said, "I would not know that, but I do know that there is no relationship between the two of them."

Frieler asked, "How could you know that there is no connection between your sister and the suspect?"

"My sister and I are close, very close. I know everything about Norma that a person could possibly know."

Frieler asked, "What about her husband, Gaynard? Could he have known the individual in the photo?"

Margie said, "We don't know who Gaynard knows. Norma and Gaynard have been married only seven months. We do not know everything about Gaynard, nor obviously, did Norma."

Frieler asked the same question of Jimmy and Chuck. Both of them concurred that they did not know much about Gaynard or who he might know.

Frieler asked, "Can you provide a list of relatives and friends of Norma and Inez, and anyone you can think of that knows Gaynard? The LVPD will contact those individuals to check out the story we were told by the suspect we have in custody."

Margie said, "I can provide that information, but it would be more thorough once I get home, and copy the names, addresses and phone numbers. Last week Norma and I called practically everyone we could think of looking for clues of his whereabouts. I'll get that list to you and include anyone else that could be contacted."

"That would be fine, call the information in to my office as soon as you return home."

"Can I take a photo with me to ask if anyone knows this person?"

Frieler said, "No, Mrs. Mauri we prefer that you not talk to anyone about this until the LVPD has made contact first. This is an active homicide investigation, and we do not want anyone slipping through the proverbial cracks by getting partial information. We have to be thorough in checking out his stories. If there is a connection between the suspect, the victims, or Gaynard Widick, we want to know about it before the preliminary hearing. The contact information you provide to us will be very helpful. He will likely repeat the same story to his court appointed lawyer. We want to be able to leave no doubt that he is being less than truthful.

"The suspect claims to have hitch-hiked to Las Vegas from the L.A. area. He stated that a man in a pick-up truck brought him all the way here. His arrival time line is eerily close to the same time Widick arrived in Las Vegas. We have not been able to get a trace on Widick's movements since the initial report on the truck being abandoned last week.

"We have sent out bulletins to jurisdictions in the Northwest and Southwest parts of the country. So far, we have heard nothing. We would like to know some more about Gaynard that might give us some insight as to where he has gone, or what he might be doing. We are concerned that he could also have been a victim of a homicide. What else can you tell us about him?"

Margie shifted her gaze back to her husband. "I don't know much about Gaynard. Jimmy, do you have anything you can tell the detectives?"

He shook his head, "We didn't spend a lot of time with Gaynard. Not by choice, work and kids kept us pretty busy. He and Norma would come by the house on occasion. She routinely came by to see our kids. She did that even before she got married. We saw the two of them several times, usually over dinner. He seemed quite easy going, easy to talk to, good conversations. I liked him. He seemed to fit in well amongst the family. Norma loved him, and we were happy for her. Personally, I did not see anything that would cause me to be concerned about him or his relationship with Norma. I'm afraid that neither one of us can be of much help."

"Chuck, do you have anything to add?" asked Frieler.

"Nope" Chuck swept his arm toward the Mauri's and said, "I've had less contact than they did. Are you saying there is a connection between Gaynard, and the man you have in custody?" asked Chuck.

"We don't know. We want and need to explore every possibility until we can locate, or determine, what has become of Gaynard Widick," said Detective Cooper. "We have heard from people close to him that this is highly uncharacteristic that he would somehow just up and disappear."

Chuck said, "Do you think that Gaynard picked him up and gave him a ride to Las Vegas? And, do you think Gaynard is another victim?"

Detective Frieler said, "I should have explained that a little better. We don't know if Gaynard picked up a hitch hiker or not, and we don't know if he picked up Osborn. There is a coincidence in the timing of their arrival to Las Vegas. We have to pursue the possibility that they crossed paths, and we cannot eliminate that possibility until we find Widick."

Frieler said, "We have received some information about Mr. Widick. That information came from the Alhambra PD, and some of it from Norma Widick when we spoke to her last Friday, shortly before the murders. The Alhambra PD, and the LAPD expressed concerns that Gaynard Widick may have a gambling problem, and could have run afoul with some unsavory people. But you are telling us you are not aware of any problems that he might have encountered back home?"

"That's right, we are not aware of any more than you are. Norma did share her concerns about their savings account being depleted, and the missing spare change they were saving for over a year. They placed all their loose change in a 5-gallon glass water bottle. Norma found it shattered and the money taken the day Gaynard disappeared," said Margie. "Assuming he did take that money, separating the coins, counting it all up would take time. I always imagined it would be fun for the two of them to leisurely do that at home.

"Looking back, it just seemed like a very desperate thing to do. Apparently, he might have been going to the Santa Anita Race Tracks to bet on the horses more often than anyone knew. Other than that, we don't have much of anything else to tell you. We didn't see any signs indicating something might be wrong."

Detective Cooper said, "The horse betting raised some flags after we learned about Mr. Widick taking whatever money he could get his hands on. We are only starting to learn about the dark side of gambling. We are seeing an uptick in crime, and personal problems, related to that activity. It's legal in this county, so the problems are exponentially higher than in most other places."

"We're learning that gambling causes personality changes. People withdraw, appear more nervous and are easily agitated. Other 'uncharacteristic' signs start to appear; increased smoking, increased drinking, and/or drug use. Theft becomes a problem, not unlike what happened to their savings.

"Then, lying creeps into the gambler's life. They find it increasingly difficult to keep their stories straight about where they have been or what they have been doing, and cannot accurately account for their finances. They lose the trust of their loved ones and friends. The pressure builds, and builds, until there's a breaking point. At first they try to hide it, then deny it, then lie about it, until they can't get away from their own deception any longer. The changes in behavior are subtle and may take months, even years, to surface. But when they do surface it is often too late and damage control takes over the normal day to day living. Picking up whatever pieces are left can be a daunting task.

"It's not a crime to be addicted to gambling, or drugs, or alcohol. The crime comes from the need to satisfy the addiction. Too many addicts cross the line and break the law to feed that insatiable need. The real crime, which technically is not a crime either, comes from the heartbreak that is left in the wake of the addict's pursuit to feed their addiction. The highs are short-lived. It's the anticipation that drives it on and on. An increased heart beat at the edge of the result is a booster to the system. It's physical as well as mental."

Detective Cooper went on to say, "Most people that come to Vegas are here for recreational gambling. They have set a dollar amount that they can afford to lose, and they don't go beyond that. A very few lucky ones come out ahead, but those are the exceptions. A lot of people can't quit when they are ahead, or behind; one more roll of the dice, one more pull on the slot machine, one more spin of the wheel, one more card game, and they think they will go home a winner. It doesn't work out that way. They live on the hope that they will hit a jackpot and everything will turn around for them. It's a false hope that always leads to despair.

"There is no way to tell who will get bit the hardest by the gambling bug. It knows no bounds. Someone in every age group, every race, every profession, every religion, men and women, are subject to getting bit, and then it is all downhill from there. It destroys relationships, marriages, people lose their life savings, their homes, and their jobs when that gambling bug comes indiscriminately knocking. I think you can begin to see some correlation about gambling, and what Widick might have been experiencing."

Margie said, "I can see some of that in what Norma told me about his behavior, but I personally did not spend that much time around him to see the changes. I'm trying to grasp all of this but I have not been able to get much sleep in the last 48 hours." Glancing to her right, not looking at anything but the blank wall in the meeting room, she thought, how could this happen? His betrayal is so wrong that now my mom and my sister are dead! Oh Norma, I am so sorry that none of us saw this coming. How could he do this?

A silence fell over the room for a few moments. Then Margie said, "I'm sorry if I seem a bit distracted about Gaynard's whereabouts. I'm tired and my sleep depraved mind tells me that my mother and sister would still be alive if Gaynard did not take off like he did. I really don't know what to think right now. I mostly just want to scream and cry."

"Margie, Jimmy, Chuck," said Detective Frieler. "Please accept our condolences for your loss. We know how difficult this is for you. I think those are enough questions for one day. We still need to get you to the hospital morgue to identify the bodies. At the hospital, you will also be able to make arrangements to transport your loved ones back home."

"Just one more question, if you don't mind." The detective opened a folder and pulled out a sheet of paper. He pushed it across the table and asked, "Is everything on this document correct?"

Margie and Jimmy looked it over very carefully. They confirmed the registration card for Norma's car to be correct.

The detective asked, "Is that Norma's correct name? Is that the correct make, model and year of the car? Is that her current and correct address?"

Margie and Jimmy nodded and said, "Yes, everything is correct. Where is the car?" asked Jimmy.

"It's in our impound yard. We have to keep the car and its contents for evidence until after the trial. Our forensic team will be taking samples from the car and re-constructing the murder scene by the evidence related to the vehicle."

Margie said, "We were hoping to get their personal belongings."

"I'm sorry," said the detective. "We cannot release anything at this time."

"What about the keys to Norma's house?" asked Margie. "We have to get in there and go through her things. The house key should be on her key ring. I suppose we could call a locksmith to let us in, but that seems like a lot of effort, and expense, when you have the key to the house."

The detective said, "We have to go through the house before we can let you in. There may be pertinent information on Gaynard Widick's whereabouts, or other things that will assist us in this investigation. We have asked the Alhambra Police Department to secure a search warrant for the house. They should have that by tomorrow. Someone from our department will travel to Southern California to assist in that search. Once the house is cleared as a crime scene, we can allow you in, but not before that."

Margie said, "What about my mother's things? You don't need to go through her stuff, do you? My dad still lives there and he will want me to go through her things."

"We plan on talking to your dad in the next few days when we are in Southern California. Your parent's house is not considered an active part of the crime scene but we do need to ask Mr. Malloy some questions about the Widick's, more specifically about Gaynard Widick."

Then the detective said, "It is getting late, the medical examiner will be going home in about another hour. Keep in mind, the M.E. will not release the bodies until he has conducted a full autopsy. He should be able to tell you when he expects to have completed the autopsy when we see him."

CHAPTER TWENTY

Hospital Morgue

Frieler notified the hospital morgue to let them know he would be bringing relatives of the deceased to identify the bodies. The M.E. said he would wait for them.

When they arrived at the hospital, they went directly into the administrative offices so the Mauri's would know who to talk to about transportation arrangements for their dear mother and sister.

Then the detective led the three relatives to the elevator where they would enter the morgue area on the lower level of the Las Vegas Hospital, also known as the University of Nevada Hospital. They checked in at the counter leading into the morgue area.

The detective looked at all three of them and said, "The M.E. does his best to clean up the victims, however both of them were shot in the head, execution style, and left on a desert road for several hours before a passerby discovered them. The M.E. has determined that after they were shot, the suspect drove the vehicles over their bodies as he fled the crime scene. I think you should be prepared, so you are not too shocked when you see your loved ones."

Margie, said nothing, her eyes were tearing as she struggled to hold back her fragile emotions.

Jimmy said to the detective, "I am going back upstairs, and start the paperwork to take Inez and Norma back home."

Margie and Chuck walked alongside the detective through the entry door to where the M.E. stood in front of a vault door. The morgue area appeared bright: light colored floor tiles, white walls, and lots of bright ceiling lights. Margie sensed the smell of something stronger in this room than the rest of the hospital, and assumed it to be cleaning liquids, and sterilant. Every step toward the M.E. became excruciatingly difficult. Her legs felt like they weighed tons as she took the short, but laborious steps toward the enclosures.

When they arrived at where the M.E. stood, he looked at both of them and asked "You are the daughter and you are the brother?" Both Margie and Chuck nodded.

The M.E. then turned toward the vault doors, and opened them. He pulled out a long drawer that Margie thought to be a white bed sheet covering the form of a body. He pulled out the second drawer. The same type of white sheet over the form of a body. He looked at Margie as she stared at the sheets, and gently pulled the first sheet back, and away, from the head of the body.

Margie gasped at the sight of her mother. She made an involuntary sound like a muffled scream. The body on the table, barely recognizable from the trauma of the gunshot wound, caused Margie to feel weak and nauseous. The head and face were swollen, the hair matted and discolored from the blood that gushed from the entry wound. The M.E. cleaned up the body, fairly well, but the hair and face clearly showed the matting of blood. Her skin color appeared ashen, almost the color of gray. Margie's heart broke at viewing her mother's lifeless body. Tears streaming down her cheeks, she looked at her uncle Chuck and murmured, "She does not look peaceful."

The M.E. put the sheet back over the body, then pulled back the second sheet on the other body. Margie screamed, "Oh my God, Norma!" Margie thought she might pass out or go into shock looking at the bodies of her mother and sister. Norma looked the worse, the bullet from the gun shot entered the back of her head and exited near her cheek bone just below the right eye. *My young and beautiful sister, so horrendously disfigured.* She started to fall.

Chuck reached out for his niece and drew her in beside him, supporting her.

Frieler said, "I know this is difficult. Are the two bodies Inez Malloy and Norma Widick?" Margie nodded. Chuck said yes affirming the corpses were Inez and Norma.

The detective thanked the M.E. and nodded toward Chuck and then toward the exit door. Chuck gave a gentle tug on Margie's arm to guide her out of the morgue area. She said in a soft, almost whispering voice, that she did not think would be heard, "You were right, it did not look like them, they were horribly damaged."

"I know. I'm so sorry," said the detective.

When they exited the doors, Jimmy stood waiting on the other side. He said, "I told the gal in the admin office that I would be back, I needed to be here when you came out of the morgue."

Margie took his arm for support. Jimmy could feel her trembling. The three relatives and the detective walked slowly back to the elevator.

The office personnel greeted them as they entered the office. She introduced herself as Michelle Dutro and said, "I will be helping you make all the necessary arrangements. I'm sorry for your loss."

Margie and Jimmy completed the paper work necessary to transport Inez and Norma back to Southern California. They provided the name, and phone number, of Pierce Brothers Funeral Home in Monterey Park, California. They would be receiving the bodies. Before leaving the hospital, Margie looked at Michelle and said, "Thank you, you have been very courteous and understanding as my husband and I try to make sense of what is happening. We're still in a bit of shock."

The detective drove them back to the police station and led them into the meeting room where they met earlier that day. He asked if he could be of any further assistance or answer any more question they might have.

Margie asked, "What is the next step in the trial process?"

The detective explained, "Even though the suspect is in denial of committing the crime, evidence of his guilt is pretty strong. The District Attorney will have to make the case to support the charges filed against him. The preliminary hearing is scheduled in three weeks. That is when the judge will decide if the charges warrant a trial by jury. The LVPD and county DA's office will keep you posted on the hearing dates, and we'll let you know the sentence the DA will be recommending."

"Well, hell," said Chuck. "If the S.O.B. you have in custody did this, then he deserves the needle. I'd rather it be a firing squad."

Everyone in the room sat stunned by the comment. Then the detective said, "I couldn't agree with you more. Unfortunately, I don't get to make that decision."

It seemed like an eternity, sitting in the LVPD meeting room talking to the detective about the suspect, the likely charges, and trial. When all of their questions were exhausted, they thanked the detective for his help, and stood to leave. He walked them outside to their vehicle, expressed his condolences for their loss, and told them they can contact him anytime if they have any more questions. They left the LVPD late in the afternoon, almost 5:00 p.m. Margie, still visibly shaken, wanted to get home. She wanted to see their kids, and she wanted to talk to her dad. Shocked from the horrible news and events of the last two days, she could not anticipate the news awaiting her when she entered her dad's house the next day.

CHAPTER TWENTY-ONE

Bringing Them Home

Right after Jimmy and Margie sent their two youngest kids off to school, they drove into Monterey Park to meet the funeral director and make burial arrangements. The meeting started somewhat awkwardly. The funeral director inquired about the husbands of Inez and Norma. He asked if either of them would be attending the funeral arrangement meeting.

Margie said, "This unexpected tragedy has left my dad in a fragile state of mind. I am making all the arrangements for him. I am the oldest of his three children. I identified the bodies, and I'll be the one to make the arrangements, including the burial lot locations."

"What about the spouse of Norma Widick? Is he coming in to take care of her final disposition, or has he given you authorization to do that?" he asked. "It is law in California, that the spouse will make the final decisions for funeral arrangements and disposition of the bodies, unless you have been given power of attorney. Has that happened?"

Margie told the funeral director that she does not have power of attorney from her dad or from Norma's husband. She did not like the questions; she only wanted to take care of her mother and her sister.

She said, "Norma's husband has been missing for over a week. No one knows where he is, or even if he is still alive. A missing person's report has been filed at the Alhambra Police Department. Norma is my younger sister, and she will be buried next to our dear mother. If Norma's husband turns up, and this becomes an issue, then I will take care of it at that time. It's really his fault the two of them are dead in the first place, so he's got nothing to say about it."

Margie, exhausted and emotionally drained tried to piece together everything she encountered over the past several days, nearly a week. But her mind could not grasp everything. Tired and confused about all the issues surrounding the tragedy and none of it made any sense. Things happened so fast, so suddenly, that she did not get the time to grieve. At this moment, she projected a position of authority that surprised even her husband. Extremely easy going, pleasant, cooperative, helpful, and caring, Margie became very assertive. She let everyone in that room know that this would be done her way, and no one should try to interfere. Feeling her patience too thin and her emotions too raw when she thought that Norma's husband, Gaynard, might want a different burial location and/or a different arrangement. That would not happen under any circumstance.

The funeral director nodded at her, confirming he understood, and they would move forward in meeting her requests. He then said, "I received a call from the University of Nevada Hospital regarding arrangements to move the deceased to this facility. That transfer should be completed by this afternoon." He assisted Jimmy and Margie in scripting the obituaries, the funeral service outline, and the list of pall bearers. They would need twelve. The funeral service would be held at the Catholic Church, Mission San Gabriel, where Margie's parents attended, and one of the priests would oversee the ceremony.

"Right after the service at the Catholic church, the burial will take place at the Resurrection Cemetery in Rosemead," Margie said.

Upon wrapping up the details at the funeral home, Jimmy and Margie drove to her dad's house. They wanted to see how he's doing, and if he wanted to go get some lunch before they went to the church to meet the priest and arrange for the service. They thought that the service and burial would take place on Saturday, April 4th.

PART THREE

CHAPTER TWENTY-TWO

Reckoning

The phone rang at Norma's house in Alhambra. It rang 4 or 5 times before someone answered it. A man's voice said hello over the phone.

The person making the call, on the other end of the line, paused at the sound of the voice. Then said, "Hello, this is Nancy Brockus from the insurance office, can I speak to Norma please?"

After a pause, the man's voice said, "Norma's not here, she should be at work."

Nancy Brockus hesitated again. Confused by what she just heard, she said, "I am calling from her work office, who am I speaking to?"

The man said, "This is Gaynard, her husband."

Nancy did not know what to say next. She reeled from surprise. Norma did not return to work on Monday as she said she would. Now she's talking to Norma's husband, and he sounded like he didn't know where she could be. Nancy re-introduced herself and said, "Gaynard, this is Nancy Brockus from Norma's office, she did not return to work yesterday. We have not heard from her. I am phoning her house to see if everything is alright. She said she needed to go to Las Vegas on Friday to pick up your truck which she said you left abandoned in a hotel parking lot. Norma assured me she would return to work Monday morning. But she did not show up and I grew concerned."

Gaynard felt nauseous about hearing that Norma drove to Vegas to get his truck. He thought about what a problem he created by taking off and not calling anyone, not letting anyone know where he is, and that he is alright. *What have I done?* Gaynard did not know how to respond to Nancy's inquiry as to Norma's whereabouts. He said, "I'm not sure where she is, can I have her call you back?" He did not want to go into any details or try to explain his leaving. Panic raced through his mind: *Where is Norma?*

Gaynard knew Norma would not go to Las Vegas by herself, she would have needed someone to drive the truck back. He thought it would have probably been Norma's mom and dad, or her sister and her husband, that would make the trip with her. He began to feel worse by the minute as he realized all the inconvenience he caused. He decided to call his in-laws to see if they went with Norma, or knew about her trip to Las Vegas.

About a half an hour earlier he quietly slipped into the house not expecting to find Norma at home. He assumed she would be at work. He didn't want her to confront him about his disappearance. Embarrassed and ashamed of his actions, he wanted to think about what to say.

The idea that she went to Las Vegas to get his truck came as a big surprise, and an unpleasant one. Gone for nearly 10 days, he knew that his and Norma's relationship would be in serious trouble, as well as his relationship involving other family members and friends. Ten days ago, he felt overwhelmed by the desire to go bet on the horses at Santa Anita Park and then everything fell apart.

He shattered their savings jar and took that money. He did not waste a lot of time counting the small change; nickels and dimes, but separated the quarters and fifty cent pieces. Throwing the nickels and dimes in a canvas bag, he placed them on the seat of his truck. The quarters and fifty-cent pieces weighed a lot more. Gaynard took the change into a nearby bank, and walked out that early Friday afternoon holding nearly $1,500.00 in larger bills.

He bet it all and lost it all. Feeling the need to win it back, he went to their bank, and depleted their savings account. Reasoning that he would win back the money and replace it. One of the horses he bet on placed and he won some money. Leaving Santa Anita Park that afternoon, over $3,000 in winnings, a lot less than what he lost, but he wasn't thinking about that.

Winning is an adrenalin rush, a physical and mental high that one might feel from a drug, and it pushed him on to want to win more. Heading east on the interstate, he drove his truck toward Las Vegas, expecting that his luck would continue. He gambled for the next five days until his money ran low. He took the nickels and dimes that he stuck in the rolled-up canvas bag to a cashier at the casino/hotel. The cashier gave him $400.00. He lost almost all of that the same day.

He began to think about the realization of what he's done by leaving his wife, his job, everything, to pursue a luckless, shameful, pursuit to gamble. Checking out of the Las Vegas Hotel, Gaynard went to the Greyhound bus depot where he bought a ticket to San Francisco, California. He left his vehicle in the hotel parking lot in Las Vegas.

Staying in a run-down motel outside of San Francisco, Gaynard did very little for the next several days. The thought of suicide crept into his mind as he began to feel the desperation about his losses, and having to face everyone whose trust he so blatantly violated.

His ability to logically consider his actions were de-railed. Now, he could not hide from his deceit, or the people he betrayed. There would be no reasonable explanation for his abrupt departure, abandoning his truck in Las Vegas, or why he would run north toward San Francisco. Escape consumed him and that became all he could think about.

Late Monday evening, nine days after he abruptly left his life in Alhambra, California, he walked to the Greyhound bus depot near San Francisco and bought a ticket back to Alhambra.

He got off the bus the following morning, around 9:00 a.m. He only had enough money to take a cab from the bus station to his house. When he arrived at home, he did not expect Norma to be there. He did not see her car in the driveway and assumed she left for work. Then the phone rang, and her work office wanted to know of her whereabouts. He felt in his heart that Norma would probably leave him after this incident, if she hadn't left already. He understood that no one should have to put themselves through the difficulty, the uncertainty, and the betrayal that he brought upon his wife. He felt pretty certain that his in-laws were probably not too happy about his actions either. *Norma, Norma, Norma, what have I done? I am so sorry to have brought this upon you and everyone else. I don't know what to say or how to fix it. Can you ever forgive me?* He said to himself as if he were talking to his wife.

Gaynard swallowed hard, took a deep breath, reached for the phone, and saw something he did not notice when he answered the phone just a few minutes earlier. His heart sank, already feeling nauseous, he now felt even worse. Sitting next to the phone he saw a business card from the Alhambra Police Department. He could not understand what that could be about. *Why did Norma have a business card for the local P.D.?* It began to dawn on him that his absence created a deep concern for his well-being and safety. It did not occur to him that his wife filed a missing person's report. Nervous and worried, he dialed the number to his in-law's house. His fingers were shaking as he dialed his in-laws number.

Tom Malloy answered the phone.

CHAPTER TWENTY-THREE

Shocking Phone Call

Jimmy and Margie walked into her father's house just before noon the same day. She told her father that arrangements were made for the funeral. The plan included a Saturday Memorial Church service at Mission San Gabriel and the burial at Resurrection Cemetery in Rosemead.

She told her dad, "I became a bit assertive in the conversation at the funeral home. I should have known better. I'm feeling more anger than sorrow. I'm angry at the killer and his denial. I'm growing increasingly angry toward Gaynard for leaving the way he did. I blame him for setting this whole tragic event in motion."

Tom said, "Margie, Jimmy, sit down for a minute. I have something to tell you."

The three of them took seats around the kitchen table. Tom looked directly at Margie and said, "A few hours ago, I got a phone call . . . from Gaynard."

Margie sat and stared at her dad in stunned silence.

Tom recognized his daughters' surprise by what he just told her. Not too unlike how he felt when the phone rang earlier, and Gaynard's voice came across on the other end.

Tom then faced the two of them and said, "This is by far the most difficult time of my life. My wife and my baby girl are gone forever. I am tormented by what they must have gone through. I don't know how to move forward." Tom sat silent for a moment, then said, "I was smitten with your mother the first time I laid eyes on her. We saw some difficult times, but we were always able to work things out. We were always there for each other, and we were happy."

Margie started to say something, but remained silent and listened to her dad talk.

Tom went on and said, "The pain of losing family may not go away any time soon, if it ever goes away. The news of your mother and sister being murdered has rattled me to my core.

"I feel like I'm in a free-fall that won't stop. I feel helpless. Everywhere I look, I see your mother. This is all hers. She made this our home," his arms made a sweeping motion as he looked about the house. "I expect to hear her voice every morning. I wake up thinking that she's in the kitchen making coffee.

"Right now, it is hard for me to put one foot in front of the other and keep moving. There are going to be a lot of people coming by here over the next few days. Many more will be attending the funeral. I know you are surprised and angry. I want to be angry too. I'm telling you this because I don't want any animosity to spill over during this time when we need to mourn our losses." Tears began to fill his eyes, "I am sure that Inez's siblings are feeling the same way that you do, and that this tragedy could have been avoided. I don't want to compound anyone's suffering and their grief. Not now, not at this time."

Margie continued to sit in silence. She broke her eye contact and nodded that she understood. Then she asked, "What did Gaynard say about where he's been? Does he know what happened to mom and Norma?"

Before her dad could answer, her anger returned and she said, "Under no circumstances will I allow him to interfere in the memorial service, or the burial arrangements. Norma and Mom are going to be buried next to each other."

Tom said, "I'm sure he won't interfere. He'll probably appreciate that you have taken matters into your hands and made all the necessary arrangements. I know I appreciate it. I am going to tell you what Gaynard told me about his disappearance. Please listen until I am finished, so I can get this out.

"Gaynard told me he won some money at the racetrack and then drove out to Las Vegas. He played the slots, roulette, and blackjack for days until the money dwindled to nothing. Then he bought a one-way bus ticket to San Francisco. He told me that when the last of his money dwindled, he could only afford to buy a bus ticket to come home, and face the music about his abrupt departure. He returned home around 9:00 a.m. this morning. One of Norma's co-workers called the house to find out why Norma did not return to work on Monday as planned. Gaynard answered the phone and learned that Norma drove to Vegas to pick up his abandoned truck. I think panic overcame his worry. He thought Norma might be at our house. Gaynard did not know any of the horrible things that occurred since he took off over ten days ago." Tom shook his head at how unbelievable that sounds. Then he said, "I would guess that he must have been too busy with his damn gambling to read a newspaper or watch the news on tv.

"I listened to him for a few minutes then I told him that Norma and Inez were murdered when they went to get his truck in Vegas. Gaynard became hysterical, he broke down over the phone and barely audible after hearing the bad news. Learning the results of his actions, he seemed pretty broken up. I told him he needed to call his parents, that they went with Norma and Inez to bring back the truck. Then, he needed to call the Alhambra PD as they will have a lot of questions for him. By the way he sounded, I'm not sure he could even comprehend the depth and seriousness of what I told him."

Margie said, "That does not explain a lot of things that happened."

Tom concurred and said, "That is all I know right now. More details will come out. But for now, we need to leave Gaynard to his grief, let him talk to the police, and contact his family. He's hurting too, and he's going to have to live with the consequences of what happened. I'm sure that the full impact of what he caused has not hit home yet. I would not want to be him when it does. Hell, the way this feels, I don't even want to be me right now."

"Dad," Margie said, "I will do my best to be civil around Gaynard. I probably can't speak to him at this time, so I'll avoid him." Margie hung her head and said, "I lost my mom, I lost my sister, my best friend. My children lost their grandmother and their only aunt. Two very important people in their young little lives. Two people who loved them, two people they needed, and that I needed, too." She did not want to tell her dad what the detectives told her. But it could not be postponed, it needed to happen now.

She cupped her hands to her face then looked up at her dad and said, "As difficult as this is, as painful as this feel, it is probably even worse for you. You lost a child. I don't know what I would do if I lost my husband and a child to such a senseless act. I can't imagine how people move on from the loss of a child. I'm so sorry dad."

Jimmy reached over to his wife and rubbed her upper back. He looked at Tom and said, "The LVPD has a lot of questions for Gaynard also. They want to talk to him about his possible gambling debts, and they want to know if there is any connection, or acquaintance, between him and the man they have in custody."

Tom looked surprised about Jimmy's comment. Then Margie said, "Dad, there's more." Her lips quivered as she attempted to speak, her body trembled. "Chuck wanted to be here to talk to you about this, but he could not get here until tonight or sometime tomorrow. I don't know how to tell you this," as she looked directly into her dad's eyes.

Jimmy put his hand on her arm and looked at Tom who sat completely still and silent. "Tom," he said, "The LVPD told us that the coroner determined both women were beaten, Inez may have been knocked unconscious. She had lacerations indicative of being hit repeatedly. It may have been the butt of a gun. Norma showed bruising on her arms and legs that happened before they were shot. Tom, they also told us," tears began to roll out of Jimmy's eyes as he worked on completing what he started to say, "Norma . . . he raped Norma just before he shot both of them." Jimmy looked down at the table, unable to say anymore.

Margie muttered, "Dad, I am so, so, sorry. You needed to hear this from us rather than someone else or read it in the newspaper."

No words were spoken among them for a long time, they just sat in silence, grieving and mourning. Then the phone began to ring, no one moved to answer it. Jimmy finally stood up and went to the phone. "Hello? Oh, hi Mitchell. You are calling to talk to your dad? Hold on a minute let me see if he can come to the phone."

Jimmy went back into the kitchen and told Tom that Mitchell is on the phone and if he would like to talk to him. Tom sat in his chair for a moment then stood up and laboriously shuffled toward the phone.

Michell said, "Dad, what's going on? I received a few messages that you have been trying to contact me with something urgent that you needed to talk about."

'Mitchell," said Tom, "I have some very, very bad news to tell you. I am so sorry. Where are you and can you come over?"

"Dad, tell me what's going on."

"We have been trying to reach you since Saturday. The police came to the house and said that your mother and sister were found murdered in Las Vegas early that morning," said Tom.

Mitchell said into the phone, "What? Damn it, Dad, I don't understand this! How could that happen? I'm coming over, I'll be there shortly."

Gaynard's day grew progressively worse after each contact he made. He phoned his parents right after speaking to his father-in-law. His mother's emotions were overwhelming to her. Her son returned home after a mysterious disappearance, but Gaynard's wife and mother-in-law were dead. Gaynard and his mother cried uncontrollably while on the phone together. He knew she grieved deeply over the loss of Norma, and Inez.

At his parents' encouragement, he contacted the Alhambra Police Department. They required Gaynard to meet them at the P.D. station to answer their questions. He told them he would be in as soon as he could find a ride. Calling his dad, he asked him if he could pick him up and take him to the police station.

The police were very pointed and direct in their questions. They pulled out the police report from nearly 10 days ago when Norma notified the police of a possible burglary at her house. They verified that she filed a missing person's report when he failed to come home. The police questioned him for nearly two hours to verify dates and times. They also verified that he depleted the couples savings account and where he spent his time for the past 10 days.

Before they dismissed him, they informed Gaynard that he needed to speak to a Detective Frieler at the LVPD right away. The LVPD planned to be in Alhambra later today or early tomorrow to go through Norma and Gaynard's house. The PD just secured a search warrant because the house is considered a part of the crime scene, and the police would be looking for details on Gaynard's whereabouts. The LVPD requested the search warrant and they are the lead agency on the murders.

The seriousness of his actions began to weigh heavily on him. Gaynard left the police station distraught and broken. The impact of his weak explanation about why he disappeared hit home with the seriousness of the police questions. Two people are dead: how do you explain that?

He did not know where to go after he walked out of the police department. Going back to their rental home in Alhambra frightened him. The memory of their last morning, his broken promise to see her later that day so the two of them could go to dinner, haunted him. She's gone forever, and he could not bring himself to return to the house where his betrayal began and ended in the loss of his beloved's life. Gaynard asked his parents if he could stay at their place for a few days until he could sort things out. It shook him to learn from the Alhambra P.D. that he is a person of interest and the police considered the house a crime scene and they would be conducting a search of the premise.

From his parents' house, Gaynard called the LVPD. The operator transferred him to Detective Frieler. The detective said, "Hello Mr. Widick. We have been looking for you for several days. Two of our LVPD detectives will be in Alhambra today to do a search of your residence. We will be conducting that search in cooperation with the Alhambra PD. How soon can you be back in Las Vegas to see me? I have a lot of questions for you, so the sooner we can meet, the sooner you can start to clear things up."

"I will leave first thing tomorrow morning."

Then Gaynard asked his dad if he felt like taking another trip to Vegas. "I'm not sure I can make the drive alone," said Gaynard.

"Of course, I don't think you should be alone at this time." Father and son arrived in Las Vegas just before noon the following day.

Gaynard's conversation with the LVPD proved to be even more difficult than the one at the Alhambra Police Department. Detective Frieler interrogated him as much as he interrogated the murder suspect. The LVPD would not clear Gaynard of any wrong doing in their initial meeting. They told him they intended to follow up on every story, and every detail, and every individual's name that he gave them. They questioned him about his wife's life insurance policy, and if he, at any time contacted, or knew the suspect in custody. Gaynard became visibly shaken by the questions insinuating that he might know the suspect or have anything to do with the killings.

Gaynard thought, I cannot believe any of this has happened. It might as well have been me that did this. I set the whole thing in motion when I ran off.

"Am I going to need a lawyer?"

"That is probably a good idea," said the detective.

Gaynard unleashed a nightmare upon himself that only just begun.

CHAPTER TWENTY-FOUR

Closure?

Closure: An act of closing. The condition of being closed. An often comforting or satisfying sense of finality // victims need closure.

Merriam-Webster

The day before the funeral service, family members and close friends gathered at Tom Malloy's house. All of Inez's siblings were there. Her oldest brother, Buster, and his wife Bev, were going to take a train, but decided to drive. They brought Inez's elderly dad, Henry. Inez's younger sister, Dorothy, and her husband, Lloyd, also made the trip from Idaho.

Lots of young kids were running and playing in the yard. Someone fired up the barbecue and just about everyone brought something for the others to eat. Margie proved to be a gracious hostess. She greeted everyone, catching up with people she did not get to see or talk to in a long time. Tom, having not seen his father-in-law, Henry, or his brother-in-law, Buster, in over two years looked forward to talking to them. Gaynard did not attend.

Henry, sat down in a chair next to Tom. He asked, "Tom, how are you holding up?"

"Not well, to tell the truth, I'm not getting much sleep."

Henry said, "I remember when Inez's mom took ill. Carrie's health slowly went downhill over several years. Then the three boys all went off to war. I remember how gut wrenching and heartbreaking the news when we were told that Louie had been shot behind enemy lines. I thought I would lose Carrie then. Louie survived and remained in active duty. Carrie's spirits lifted and somehow she hung on until all three of our boys made it home at the end of the war. The following month she passed. It seemed as if she hung on just long enough to see her boys come back home. Losing her proved to be difficult, but I had time to prepare for it. All of her kids, relatives, and friends were able to say goodbye. An unforgettable sad time, but we found closure. Losing one of her children would have been the worst thing that could have happened to her.

"You lost your wife and daughter, my daughter and granddaughter, in an unimaginable way. I'm sorry there are not any words of comfort that would ease what you are feeling. It eases a bit, but it's always there. It doesn't matter how old they are, you always want them to be safe, and healthy."

Tom understood what his father-in-law said. Norma's an adult, but she's my kid. She would always be my kid, no matter what her age. Inez is still Henry's kid, and he misses her too. Tom wondered, *Is closure possible? They were taken too soon, too tragically, too abruptly. I don't know if I can put this behind me and move on—ever. The wound is too new, too raw. The old adage: time heals all wounds, might not apply this time; they were stolen from me, ripped away.*

Inez's siblings and other relatives gathered in the living room of Tom's house that he and Inez shared since they moved to California. Everyone began to tell stories and share memories about their sister. Once the stories started, laughter and more stories followed.

They reminisced about four of the siblings uprooting their families and following Inez to California.

Vera, the oldest of the siblings said, "I remember the chores we each needed to do. Buster" she said, looking at her brother, "you were the oldest of the boys, and the ringleader troublemaker." She giggled and said, "Do you remember the time that Louie drew the wrath of us girls because we were tasked with the laundry duties. You thought it to be pretty funny to pee on Louie's bed and watch us girls get mad at him. How old was he then, three, maybe four? Then Inez spotted the tell-tale signs of your shenanigans: you left a drip line going back to where you and Chuck were standing.

Then one morning when Louie came down for breakfast, she put her finger in front of her lips to let me know to be quiet. Then she silently motioned for me to follow her up the stairs. Quiet as a mouse, we made our way to the door of the boys' bedroom. We saw Chuck and Buster standing on the foot of the bed. And what were they doing? Peeing where Louie slept so he would get in trouble for wetting the bed. Inez told me to be quiet and we made our way back down stairs. Chuck and Buster came down to join everyone for breakfast and acted like nothing happened.

"I don't know what Inez did, but she must have horded some very hot spices or a chili. She placed a plate of scrambled eggs in front of you two hellions and they began to scarf it down. Almost at the same time they both reached for their milk. Then they jumped up out of their chairs and went to the sink and began splashing water in their mouths. When you could finally talk, you asked what is in those eggs, they are too hot to eat. No one said anything, we were all shocked and amused at the scene that just unfolded. Inez looked at Louie and said, I think we found the culprits. Then Louie and Chuck tore out through the back door as though nothing happened. She looked at Buster, accused him being the ring leader of the fiasco and told him it better not happen again. He protested and wanted to know why he's getting blamed when it could have been Chuck's idea. Inez told you that Chuck is barely 5 years old. He's too young to think of that bad idea. Inez bowed her head, stared straight at Buster and said this is the end of it. And it never happened again."

"Yeah," Buster said laughing. "Inez would always bail us out when we were in trouble for our mischief. But when she put her foot down, we knew to get in line and be quick about it."

The laughter grew loud as stories and fond memories of Inez and Norma continued for hours.

Then they were interrupted by a phone call as they were talking and reminiscing about Inez and Norma. Margie's Uncle Chuck sat in the chair at the doorway to the kitchen, nearest to the phone. He started to get out of the chair and step away from the phone when Margie asked him if he would answer it. She could tell by the expression on his face that he did not want to do it.

He picked it up, and said, "Yeah?"

The man's voice on the other end said, "Who is this?"

Chuck said, "Well, who do you want?"

"I want to talk to my dad!" said the voice on the phone.

"Mitchell?" asked Chuck.

"Yes." He answered.

"This is Chuck, where in the hell are you?"

"I'm calling to see if I can get a ride. I've been detained for a traffic violation. Would you put my dad on the phone?" asked Mitchell.

"Where are you?" asked Chuck again.

"I'm at the L.A. County Sheriff's station in Pasadena. I have to post bail, so they'll let me go. Now, will you put my dad on?"

"You sit tight a while longer; I'll come get you." Chuck hung up the phone, glanced around the room and said he's heading to get Mitchell because he needed a ride.

As he started out the front door, Tom hollered to him, "Chuck, where you going?"

"Mitchell just called, he's having car trouble and needs a ride. I'm going to fetch him, be right back."

Tom raised his hand in a gesture that said, *see you soon.*

CHAPTER TWENTY-FIVE

Dead End Street

The clerk at the jail told Chuck that the bail fee is $100.00. Chuck counted out the money and asked, "What kind of a moving violation landed him in the pokey?"

The clerk glanced across the counter and said, "It has nothing to do about a traffic violation, if that's what you're asking. He punched his girlfriend, and she asked for our assistance. It's not the first time either. She has filed a restraining order. He landed here because he became too belligerent toward the officers. Seems he has a problem keeping his mouth shut when he should, not to mention keeping his hands to himself."

The clerk pushed a piece of paper across the counter and said, "There is a restraining order against Thomas Mitchell Malloy. If you're taking him home, you don't want to take him to this address. He's not allowed to be within 500 feet of the residence, or his girlfriend. Just so you know, if you drop him off there, and we have to go back, you would've *assisted* him in violating the restraining order. And then, we would have to talk to *you* also."

Chuck and Mitchell walked out of the sheriff's station to the pick-up truck.

Mitchell said, "Thanks for getting me out."

Chuck asked him, "What kind of moving violation did you get that landed you in jail?"

"Too many parking tickets," Mitchell said. "Can you take me back to my house, so I can get my car?"

"Where would that be?" Chuck asked.

"Right here in Pasadena, I'll show you how to get there."

About three miles down the road, Chuck made a right-hand turn; not in the direction that Mitchell gave him. He turned down a dead-end street, drove to the end of the street, made a U-turn, and parked the truck. Chuck got out, walked to the front of the truck and pulled out a pack of cigarettes. He tapped the pack of Lucky Strike until a cigarette popped out, he lit it, leaned against the truck, and began to smoke.

Mitchell yelled out the passenger window, "Hey, what are you doing? I want to get home."

Chuck ignored him and continued to smoke.

Mitchell got out of the truck and walked up to Chuck. He put his hand out, palm up, and said, "I'll drive, give me the keys, and you can have your smoke."

Chuck took another drag on his cigarette, exhaled, and said, "I don't think so. Tell me again why the police collared you."

Mitchell felt his anger rising. He did not want to be questioned—by anybody, about anything. Then he thought about all the stories his dad told him about his Uncle Chuck. He's not a patient man, but he would do anything for you. He would give you the shirt off his back, if you asked for it. But if you tried to take it, that would likely be your last conscious thought. *Shit, he's going to make an issue out of this, and there's nothing I can do about it.*

Mitchell resigned himself to the fact that he will have to talk to his uncle. He took a deep breath and leaned his back against the truck. He did not look at Chuck when he finally began to talk.

"I cannot put my finger on what is bothering me. Whatever it is, it has been eating at me for years. I don't mean for my hostility to be aimed at any one person. I especially do not have anything against you. You have always been fair with me. I've never fit in, Chuck. I have never fit in. If I think about it, I really can't blame anyone else. When Dad told me what happened to Mom and Norma, I lost it. I struck my girlfriend—she called the cops. I know that they told you what happened, and that's why we're killing time on this dead-end street."

"That's not the only reason we're here," Chuck said. "You have been acting out for quite a while, for too long. I am not sure what in the hell is all going on in your world, but I can tell you that your dad is going through more pain and suffering right now than any human being should ever have to go through.

"Margie's carrying the brunt of picking up the pieces to this mess. You're not helping and I am getting the impression that you don't want to help. I feel like beating some sense into you, but I don't know what good that would do.

"I am *not* taking you back to your house. There's a restraining order against you, which says you cannot go there. If you end up back there, you'd be better off in police custody than having me talk to you again. I'm taking you to your dad's house. He does not know you were arrested. I didn't tell him, and he doesn't need to know. If he found out you hit that girl, I'm not sure what he would do. He's suppressing a lot of anger right now, don't give him an excuse to take it out on you. No one would blame him if you ended up eating through a straw for a long time. You are going to straighten up and fly right. Am I clear on that?"

"Yeah, you're clear" Mitchell said. "But I don't think you understand. I never got to say goodbye to my mom, or my sister. I have not seen them for months. Now I will never see them again."

"Oh, I understand," said Chuck. "What I don't understand is why in hell you've chosen the path that you're on. You're probably going to do whatever it is that you want to do. You are throwing away an opportunity that most people would jump at having."

"What opportunity? What are you talking about?" said Mitchell.

Chuck did not tell Mitchell that he knew about his working at a porn shop in L.A. and that he suspected he might be involved in drug use and maybe selling drugs.

"Your dad and mother have created a very successful dry-cleaning business. I think they both believed you would take over the operation, but you don't seem to want to have any part in it. In addition to Inez and Norma being murdered, your dad is showing signs of schizophrenia. No one knows if that will get worse, but I doubt that he can manage on his own without your mother being there."

Mitchell sighed, hesitated before saying anything. "I can't do that. I never did like the dry- cleaning business. My dad would take me to work to the business almost every weekend when I was home, sometimes after school on the weekdays. I didn't like the smell of it, and I did not like any part of being there. My dad put a lot of pressure on me to work the business. He expected that I would someday take over. I am not interested, I never will be. That has probably added to the rift between my dad and me. But, I have to do what *I* want to do, not what anyone else thinks I should be doing. I know he thinks someone has been watching the house, I'm not the guy that can fix that either.

Then Chuck said, "I doubt that anything will change your mind about what you are doing. Watch your step and don't cause your dad any more trouble. One more thing, your dad has laid down the law to all of us that we are not to take this out on Gaynard. That will be honored, no matter how anyone feels. By the way, you owe me a hundred bucks for bailing you out of jail. You don't have to pay it right now, but I am expecting it when you have it."

Mitchell said, "I'll pay you back, and I don't blame Gaynard. He has his demons too, and he has to face this bad memory, maybe for the rest of his life, not unlike me." Mitchell thought about his sister, Norma, then he said, "Norma is probably the nicest person I have ever known. She's always been a good sister to me, and I ignored her. She never bothered me, never judged me. Always happy, I don't think I ever felt happy like Norma did. And I didn't give her the time of day." Mitchell became silent. Then in a quiet voice he said, "They didn't deserve what they got."

Chuck responded and said, "No they did not. No one deserves what happened to them, except maybe the son-of-a-bitch that did this." Chuck never told anyone, including Mitchell, about the horrific circumstances that Inez and Norma encountered on the night of the murders. He did let his brother Louie know of the hell the two women went through. He did not feel it necessary to share their hell with anyone else. Tom or Margie could do that, if they wanted to. It would probably all come out in court anyway. He took one last drag on his cigarette and crushed it out under his foot. Then he said, "C'mon, get in the truck, I'm taking you to your dad's house. Do we need to stop at a store and pick anything up for you?"

Mitchell said, "No, I'll be fine." He relaxed against the truck and said, "I appreciate what you are trying to do. I'm glad you did not tell my dad about me being arrested. He doesn't need to know that.

"My mom talked about you and Uncle Louie quite a bit. She always said the two of you can do anything. Nothing that broke would stay broken if Louie or Chuck were to come around. I think Uncle Louie got under her skin more than anyone. She labeled him as the daredevil in the family, no fear of anything. It always made her mad. I remember that as a kid and I remember how solemn she became when she heard that Louie had been shot in the war jumping behind enemy lines. He came home with a Purple Heart. She said that he couldn't join up right away, too young, he needed to wait six more months. She said you waited six months for him so the two of you could go in together. She would shake her head in disbelief because he went into the paratroopers, and ended up being shot. She worried about him, about all of you; she cared a lot. She cared about everybody. Damn it, Mom and Norma being murdered, doesn't seem real."

Mitchell failed to take the opportunity to unveil some very important information that he kept from his immediate family and extended family. No one would know about his secret for a long, long time.

CHAPTER TWENTY-SIX

Saying Good-Bye

S everal family members and close friends arrived at Tom's house a few hours
before the Mass and funeral at Mission San Gabriel.

Gaynard received a call from Tom Malloy regarding the gathering of
friends and relatives prior to the Mass. He invited Gaynard to attend, and
he did. He did not appear to be doing well, and neither did Tom. Glaringly
obvious that they were both having a tough time of daily life without their
wives. Tom asked Gaynard, "Are you getting any sleep?"

Gaynard replied, "maybe an hour." He stood by himself, off to one side
of the living room, smoking a cigarette that he replaced with another as soon
as it ran low. He looked frail and his hands were shaking. The light gray suit
he wore hung on his frame, making it obvious he lost some weight.

Tom's wishes that everyone be cordial, and not accusatory about Gaynard's
actions in the past two weeks were honored. Some in attendance went out of
their way to engage Gaynard in conversation. Even so, Gaynard appeared to
be uncomfortable, nervous, and found it difficult to make eye contact.

Around noon, the crowd at Tom's house began to leave for the church service.
Tom and Inez were members of this church since they moved to California,
more than ten years ago. The crowd of mourners were larger than the seating
pews could accommodate. Over 500 people were in attendance. Many of them
stood along the walls of the interior of the church during the Mass. Norma and
Inez touched many lives and made a lot of friends in the San Gabriel Valley area.

The caskets were set in the front of the church, just below the raised dais where the priest conducted the service. Because of the damage caused by the gunshot wounds to their heads, the lids to the caskets were closed. A large, beautiful portrait of both women were placed next to their caskets.

The Catholic church conducted most of the funeral services in Latin, a practice they employed for centuries. Even though the priest used a language that very few could understand, the attendees understood the meaning of what the priest conveyed. Solemn, but uplifting, while honoring the loss of the two women. A universal message, regardless of the language.

After the Mass, the crowd filed outside, into the parking lot, and drove in a long funeral procession to the cemetery. The line of cars stretched for over a mile, and the local police department provided traffic control through the intersections.

Nearly all the people in attendance at the service mass were again in attendance for the burial service at the Resurrection Catholic Cemetery. This burial service did not last long, about 30 minutes. The Catholic Priest said a few words over the caskets before they were lowered into the ground. Then the mourners walked back to their cars to go home and resume their lives without their two close friends. All of Inez's family went back to Tom's house for most of the afternoon.

Back at Tom's house, he and Margie, explained what they knew about the details of the murder to the family members that were not up to date on everything. Tom, at times, would hesitate in his description of the situation. It became obvious that talking about the murders pained him. He would stop in mid-sentence, struggling to find the words. Margie continued the conversation when she noticed her dad struggling to talk about the killings.

Every gamut of emotion: sadness, shock, anger, silence, and disbelief could be observed as Tom and Margie told their relatives what they knew about this horrific and senseless act of murder.

Tom told his relatives that the LVPD arrested a suspect on first degree murder charges. The suspect continues deny any involvement in the killings. He has a criminal record, including a 5-year prison sentence in Oregon. He went on to let everyone know that there will be a preliminary hearing soon, and that will determine if the evidence is strong enough to have a full-blown trial by a jury of his peers. The LVPD is certain that it will happen and the evidence will be enough to convict the accused of the homicides.

The approaching preliminary hearing created more drama, and would push Tom deeper into depression.

CHAPTER TWENTY-SEVEN

Interrogatory Debacle

When the Clark County Sheriff's Deputy hauled the suspect in before the Las Vegas Justice of the Peace, Roger Bradshaw, for his initial hearing, he told the JP that he intended to represent himself at any pending hearing. The JP reminded the defendant that he appointed a defense attorney to assure the courts and the defendant that his constitutional rights were not being violated. The JP went on to say, "By defending yourself there is a higher risk that something would certainly go wrong during the trial. I want to avoid an appeal that is prompted by a lack of defense on your behalf. Thus, I have appointed defense counsel to assist you recognizing that you have the right to represent yourself. I strongly urge against that."

Two preliminary hearings were scheduled; one for Inez Malloy's murder, and one for the murder of Norma Widick.

The defendant and the court-appointed defense attorney met prior to the first scheduled preliminary hearing set for June 5th. Defendant Osborn told his attorney he did not want him to make any opening or closing statements. When the time came, and if Osborn deemed it necessary, he would speak for himself. Objections and/ or questions would also be addressed by Osborn, not the court appointed attorney.

"The JP informed me of your intentions and requested that I be on hand in the event you stray too far outside the legal court proceedings. I know a few things about you and your run-ins with the law. I can assure you that learning, or hearing, legal proceedings from a jail cell or prison is not the same as being there," said the court appointed attorney.

Osborn bristled at the comment. "I do not want you there *at all*. I do not intend to ask for your help. If I feel you are interfering in my defense, you should know that I have the right to have you removed. You know that, don't you, counselor?"

The attorney studied Osborn for a moment, then said, "By the way, my name is Lance Bridges. You can call me Lance. I understand that you also spoke to the District Judge, Zenoff, prior to my appointment. He concurred that you have the right to defend yourself in a capital trial, but he, too, wants to make sure your constitutional rights are not trampled upon."

"Those are my rules," said Osborn. "I do the talking."

"Have it your way. You know why I'm here and what my role is in this trial."

On the day of the first preliminary hearing, Tom, Margie, Jimmy, Chuck and about a dozen other family members were seated behind the DA. Osborn, led into the courtroom in handcuffs and shackles, sat at the defense table.

Chuck watched the killer be seated and said to his relatives, "Well, well, well, what do we have here? It appears the county provided him with a suit and tie. His hair's been cut and trimmed, and his face is clean shaven. A stark contrast to his mug shot right after his arrest. He could be mistaken for a business man, or another attorney at the defense table. He doesn't look like the hell-bent, chicken-shit killer that he is."

Oddly, during the first preliminary hearing, Osborn did not raise any questions. He also did not seek any input from his court appointed attorney. He silently sat at the defense table and took copious notes.

On June 5th, the evidence brought forward in the first hearing, the murder of Inez Malloy, deemed sufficient enough to compel the justice of the peace to determine that there is probable cause that Roy Warren Osborn committed the crime of first-degree murder of Inez Malloy. The accused would be held in custody for a capital trial.

The second hearing, held on June 16th for the murder of Norma Widick, took unexpected turns at almost every part of the hearing. The Assistant DA needed to prove again that the murder of Norma Widick, like that of her mother, has sufficient supporting evidence to move the trial into superior court for a trial by jury on the crimes committed.

Before the second preliminary hearing began, the defendant sent a letter to Chief Justice Zenoff of Clark County. The judge made the letter and his response to the letter available to the prosecution and the defense.

"The Supreme Court allows for the defendant to have counsel for homicide charges. There are two hearings scheduled. I should have counsel for both of them and I want separate counsel for each hearing." Osborn went on to say, "The pending hearing would address both homicide charges on two separate dates. I do not have counsel for the second hearing against me. What are you going to do about that?"

The Chief Justice reviewed the charges and the documents from the initial appearance. He noticed that the defendant insisted that he be allowed to represent himself at the preliminary hearing. Now he wants two different attorneys to represent him for each of the two murder charges. The Chief Justice responded by saying, "The court appointed attorney assigned to you at the first preliminary hearing, is there for the purpose of assisting you in this case, and to protect your rights. The court appointed attorney will represent you in both hearings in front of the justice of the peace. The appointment of the attorney assures you of your constitutional rights."

The chief justice recognized that the defendant found himself overwhelmed by the evidence brought against him during the first preliminary hearing concerning the murder of Inez Malloy. The judge always discourages anyone from attempting to represent themselves in the courtroom. It can be both confusing and intimidating. This latest turn of events regarding the defendant signaled that Osborn wants legal representation, even more than is required.

The JP banged his gavel on the desk and the second hearing came to order on June 16th. Immediately the defense attorney and the defendant objected to the proceedings. "The defendant has the right to allow, or not allow, any witnesses in the courtroom. We want all parties not representing the defendant, or the prosecutor's office staff to be removed," said the defense counsel.

The JP concurred that this would be a closed hearing and everyone would be removed except for the bailiff, court reporter, and legal counsel. The media followed the court case very closely. Today, not even family members or the media would be allowed in the courtroom.

After the courtroom cleared of everyone not associated with the defense or the prosecution, the defense counsel objected again. "My client is not prepared for this hearing because he has not been provided a pencil and paper by which to take notes."

The JP overruled the objection. Pausing for a moment, he told the defense and the prosecution that he did not want to see silly, or frivolous, objections throughout the hearing. Then he ordered the proceedings to continue.

"Your Honor," said the counsel for the defendant as he stood up out of his chair, "My client has not been afforded sufficient time to prepare for this preliminary hearing, and neither have I. Allow me to bring to the attention of the court that my client has been detained at the Clark County Sheriff's station. He has not been able to travel freely in order to adequately respond to the charges brought by the DA's office. We request that the preliminary hearing be postponed until such time that the defendant, and defense counsel, can prepare a sound defense. We request that you have the DA's office submit interrogatories to the defendant so he can review them and respond to them from his jail cell. The defendant, we request, should also be allowed to submit questions to the DA in which the DA should respond, in kind, before we enter into this second preliminary hearing."

Assistant DA, Edna Lingreen, immediately objected and stated, "Your Honor, that is ludicrous. We cannot conduct a hearing based on interrogatories that are responded to from a jail cell."

"Not so fast," said the JP. "The court is obligated to hold a fair trial and provide full disclosure of evidence so the defendant knows how to respond. In this case, the defendant has pleaded not guilty, and he deserves to know the extent of the charges brought against him. This will allow the defendant to respond to your office, in writing, and ask questions of his own in such a high-profile capital crime case."

"Your Honor," said Lingreen, "such a request would set this case back several months, probably longer. The idea of submitting my questions to the defendant outside of the courtroom is unprecedented. The back, and forth, of questions and answers, could potentially drag on indefinitely. If such an allowance were to occur it would set all court cases back for months, if not years. The defendant and his attorney, know why they are here. We have gone through this at the initial appearance, and the discovery period, so they would know of our intent to prosecute for this heinous crime.

"My task, and the task of the state, is to prove to the court of the people that the defendant committed the crime. We are not tasked, and it is not our responsibility to prove to the defendant what he did, or why he is being charged. That has already occurred at the time of the defendant's arrest and you repeated it to him at his initial appearance and arraignment.

"Written questions were given to the defense counsel regarding the defendants' whereabouts on the night of the crime, his association with the victim, or victims, how he came into possession of the car, along with other preliminary hearing questions. That is a standard practice in the trial process, some questions are expected to be answered, in writing, and under oath, prior to the hearings.

"The number of questions, presented by either side, is limited by court rule. Clark County, and the State of Nevada, has set that number of questions to not exceed twenty-five. The court has appointed a defense lawyer to advise him through the course of this hearing. Defense counsel knows the intent of interrogatories. I am quite surprised that the defense would suggest such a procedure.

"The interpretation that you are suggesting for the use of interrogatories would likely create a never-ending saga of questions, and answers, that are intended for the courtroom. The number of written questions could potentially be in the hundreds, if not thousands. Next, the defense will undoubtedly want to ask questions of the expert witnesses in writing, responses in writing, under oath, and the charade will continue without purpose, and without an end."

The JP listened intently to the impassioned speech by the prosecution. He sat back in his chair, leaning to one side resting on his elbow. Then he said, "I concur that proceeding with the preliminary hearing through interrogatories could add several months onto the case. I am also aware of the recommended set number of interrogatory questions. However, that number can be increased by the court.

"It is nearly lunchtime, and we have already been bogged down in courtroom proceedings. I am going to recess the hearing for lunch and will give you my decision as soon as we return."

The assistant DA stared intently at the JP for several moments. *You have never practiced law, nor have you ever attended law school, have you?* She pondered the question but did not ask it.

Lingreens' assistant sat at the table next to Lingreen throughout the hearing. Jolie Eimers placed both of her hands, palms down, on the table in front of her. Positioning herself to push back from the table and stand up. But she did not move, she continued to sit at the table, staring at the dais where the JP just vacated his seat.

Lingreen turned slightly in her chair and gazed at her young assistant without saying anything. Jolie could sense Lingreen staring at her then she said, "I am trying to sort this out. The JP is going to rule on the use of interrogatories right after lunch. However, his interpretation contradicts everything I learned in law school about the purpose and intent of interrogatories. The process, as presented by the justice of the peace, would allow for the proceedings to be conducted in a manner that may just remove this hearing, this trial, from the courtroom. It sounded like the JP would have us present our questions on paper, and send them to the jail where the defendant can answer—also in writing. The defendant may also send back cross-interrogatories making the proceedings of the preliminary hearing like that of a court trial, only it will be done in writing, and from the prisoner's jail cell. It's unheard of."

"Yes, you have that correct," said Lingreen. "This is going to be more interesting than I anticipated. Let's get a quick lunch and hear what the JP has to say about this when he reconvenes the hearing."

The JP reconvened the court shortly after 1:00 p.m.

"I will allow the defense request to have interrogatories sent to the defendant's jail cell where he can respond to them in writing. He can seek assistance from his attorney, or not, since he invoked his right to defend himself. Every response will be made under oath and recorded."

Assistant DA, Lingreen, stood up to address the JP and said, "Your Honor, allow me to go on record of requesting an opinion from the State Attorney General's office on the intended use, and interpretation, of interrogatories before we proceed any further on this hearing. No dis-respect intended, but this ruling, or interpretation coming from the bench, could potentially set the Nevada Judicial System on its ear. Every case would be bantered back and forth through the defendants' jail cell. I am sure that before we leave this courtroom today, other prisoners will learn of this decision, and they too will be making the same requests of the court."

"We will proceed, as outlined, and I will allow for you to seek an opinion from the State Attorney General," said the JP. "Are there any more questions, or objections, from the prosecutors table, or the defense table? If not, then we will adjourn until such time that the defense has seen, and responded to the DA's questions."

Just before the JP could bring down the gavel and adjourn the court, the defense made another request.

"Your Honor," said the defense lawyer, "my client would also like copies of all the court transcripts sent to his jail cell for his perusal."

The Assistant DA objected again saying, "No. We will not pay for that. My office is not going to hire a court reporter and have the transcripts prepared in a written form, copied, and sent to the prisoner. It is not in the prosecutor's budget. Every question proposed under your interpretation of interrogatories will require a court reporter to record every question, and every answer to those questions has to be done under oath, even if it is in writing. My office strenuously objects to the hearing proceeding until we receive an opinion on the use of interrogatories by the state attorney general."

The JP over ruled the objection. He said, "The prisoner should be entitled to court transcripts, if this is simply a budgetary issue, the cost can come out of my budget until such time that the DA's office and the court can come to terms." Then the JP adjourned the hearing. There were no opening arguments, or presentation of any evidence on the first day of the second preliminary hearing; the murder of Norma Widick. The court adjourned at mid-afternoon in expectation that the state attorney general's office would soon rule on the issue of interrogatories.

Before leaving the courtroom, Assistant DA Lingreen leaned closer to her office assistant so what she told her could only be heard by Jolie. "A request by the defense to have the prosecution submit their interrogatory questions is out of the ordinary. It is an unprecedented approach by the defense that should not have been given the consideration that it received. It is a clear mis-interpretation of the intent of the law. Allowing, or worse yet; participating in this ruling could bring the Nevada judicial system to the verge of unraveling. At the moment I am leaning toward asking the attorney general to intervene until this can be thoroughly vetted."

Jolie nodded her head indicating she understood the dilemma. The two of them exited the courtroom.

CHAPTER TWENTY-EIGHT

Frustration without End

T he Assistant DA Lingreen felt more frustrated than she could remember during any of her past hearings or trials.

District Attorney Gould, Assistant DA Lingreen, and key staff members from the DA's office held a de-briefing when Lingreen and Eimers returned from the courtroom. Lingreen reflected on how smooth everything went in the first preliminary hearing, barely a wrinkle in the first prelim. Her findings and evidence presented to the court received very little response from the defense or the JP. The evidence presented convinced the JP to hold the suspect for jury trial on homicide charges, and to be held without bond. Now, the second hearing involving the same suspect, same crime, same JP, involving a second victim, and the same evidence has run into unprecedented twists, turns and delays.

A troubling concern that Lingreen could not dismiss was the fact that this crime, now in the preliminary hearing stages, would be heard by a JP. They often sit in on the initial appearance to determine if the charges brought against a suspect should move forward to a preliminary hearing. However, at that time, a district judge assigned a JP to hear the charges. JP's historically do not hear capital criminal cases. They handle speeding violations, careless driving, disturbances of the peace. *How could this case have proceeded without the proper judicial oversight that it requires,* she questioned. More disturbing to her, is that the defense attorney, and/or the defendant, convinced the JP to ignore the legal intent of the interrogatories, making a circus out of the proceedings.

She recognized that the defendant and his counsel were well aware after the first hearing, that this case would go to trial. She also knew the court-appointed attorney lacked experience trying a capital case. On the other hand, she has prosecuted many felony cases. She understood that every road block, every delay, would buy time for the defense to build a case to avoid a trial.

During the first prelim, the defense did not attempt to impeach even one of the qualified witnesses that she brought in to testify. The supporting documentation by experts did not hear any challenges. This time she needed to be prepared that every witness, and every piece of evidence would be questioned. The defense already attempted to have the case thrown out for what they alleged as an illegal search and seizure of the victims' car. They might try to bring that up again, she thought.

The DA's office filed a formal request for review of interrogatories by the State Attorney General, citing inevitable delays in the hearing process. The law never intended for the prosecution to submit their questions, or entire case, to the defendant ahead of a hearing, or a trial.

The Assistant DA took another step, and requested that the JP presiding over the preliminary hearing be replaced by a district judge. She knew that by doing this it would create an adversarial situation between the DA's office, and the current presiding JP. She knew that a supporting recommendation on the interrogatories issue from the state Attorney General would likely cause a bit of a rift between her and the JP. If her request to replace the JP by a district judge were denied, and the JP were to remain on the case, the Assistant DA felt that she would be put at a disadvantage going forward. She also thought that the case of a double homicide, even the preliminary hearing, should be held in the courtroom of a district judge, not a justice of the peace.

Lingreen felt that it became necessary to contact the victims' husband and father, Tom Malloy, and apprise him of the delay in the second preliminary hearing. She informed Tom that the case hit an unexpected roadblock before it got through the first day. The hearing would more than likely be put on hold until a review and opinion, from the State Attorney General's office could be addressed before the court regarding the interpretation of interrogatories. She added that she could be held in contempt of the court if she does not comply with the directive from the JP. However, her office is requesting that the State Attorney General intercede until he can render an opinion.

Tom asked, "How long will that take?"

"My hope is that it doesn't take any longer than a few days, but it could take a couple of weeks," said Lingreen. "I'm confident that the opinion will be favorable. This particular JP does not have a law degree, and has, in my opinion, loosely interpreted the intent of interrogatories, which is at the core of the delay. It is not just this case that will be set back, but every felony case and probably misdemeanor cases, in the state of Nevada. It is a far-reaching move by the defense, and I don't think it has much of a chance of holding up. But nonetheless, it has been brought up and now the court has to address the issue."

Tom expressed his disappointment, but he knew that expressing his concerns would not accomplish anything. The nightmare of the murders and any possible conclusion would be put on hold. *There's no such thing as being put on hold, this nightmare grinds on relentlessly, day in and day out.* After the call ended, Tom talked to Margie to let her know about the drama that unfolded in the courtroom.

No one expected the review on the interpretation of interrogatories to last as long as it did. Nearly three months passed before the State Attorney General finally rendered his opinion. He said, "This is a highly unusual interpretation by the lower courts. My review finds that the process of holding a trial through interrogatories would delay hearings far beyond the time contemplated by legislators, and it raises the constitutional question of lack of a speedy trial to which the defendant and victims are entitled to." The JP accepted the opinion of the State Attorney General and the questions requested by the defense would not be sent to the prisoner.

Regarding the request concerning court documents being provided to the defendant, the State Attorney General added, "The Clark County District Attorney's office must approve of a court reporter to be hired, and provide transcripts of the hearing to the defendant and his counsel." The DA's office accepted this opinion to provide the transcripts to the prisoner.

CHAPTER TWENTY-NINE

Capital Crime

More than five months passed since the murders occurred. A judge did not replace the JP in the preliminary hearing, much to Assistant DA Lingreen's disappointment. The defense objected to nearly every testimony and every piece of evidence submitted by the DA.

Information from expert witnesses that the DA submitted to the court included that of the forensic expert who worked at the Clark County Sheriff's office; the Medical Examiner; the LVPD forensic expert; and a couple from Portland, Oregon, who were gun collectors and sellers. They were robbery victims of the defendant. She included reports from the FBI for blood analysis testimony and ballistics testimony.

In her closing statement, Assistant DA Lingreen said, "The evidence proving the defendant's guilt in this crime is overwhelming. The people have proved beyond a reasonable doubt that the defendant committed these two homicides. In addition, Your Honor, as this hearing moves to a criminal trial, which we believe it must, the people will be seeking the death penalty of Roy Warren Osborn."

The defense counsels head snapped up when he heard the Assistant DA suggest the death penalty. The JP asked the defense if they would like to respond about his client being held over for trial based on the evidence presented by the DA's office.

The defense attorney said, "First of all, Your Honor, I am appalled at hearing the DA will seek the death penalty when they have brought such a weak case before the court. Secondly, the Assistant DA has no witnesses to the murders, and she has provided no motive to the crime. Furthermore, Your Honor, my client should not be bound over at the county jail and not be given the opportunity to post bail. That is absurd. He should be released for time served, which by the way, is over 150 days of incarceration for a crime he has repeatedly stated that he did not do, and it has not been proven by any stretch, that he did do it. I am recommending his release on his own recognizance, and that the outlandish statement by the DA's office that they will seek the death penalty be removed as any possibility."

CHAPTER THIRTY

Counsel Resignation

The justice of the peace looked at the defense counsel, then at the defendant. His eyes shifted to the lead prosecutor, and then down to the notes in front of him. After several long moments, he looked up, again glancing back and forth between the prosecution and the defense.

"Finally," he said, "there has been significant evidence presented over the course of the preliminary hearings to bind over the defendant for a criminal hearing. Reviewing the court's calendar, I am going to schedule the hearing to be moved to a criminal trial in October. There will be no bail set for the defendant. He will remain in custody until such time that a jury of his peers sets him free or convicts him." Before hitting his gavel on the desk, he asked that the prosecution and defense meet him in his chambers, and then he adjourned the preliminary hearing.

Those acting for the defense and the prosecution entered the judge's chambers. After they were seated, the JP looked at the assistant DA and said, "I asked you to be here because I wanted you to hear this."

He then looked at the defense attorney and said, "I have grown increasingly concerned about the defense you are mounting for your client, or should I say, lack of defense. You have objected to nearly every piece of evidence, and every piece of information, provided by expert witnesses, even when the evidence was damning, and the expert witnesses' credentials were outstanding. What you have not done is to provide any sound basis to impeach witness testimony or findings of evidence. If a jury convicts the defendant of first-degree murder, then capital punishment becomes a possibility. Your client needs more than verbal objections, that won't get him out of the trouble he is heading into. I do not want to debate your strategy, but if that is all you have to offer, you're going to lose this case, and your client might lose his life. The crimes that your client has been charged with would almost always lead to a jury trial. Your trial records indicate you have not yet defended a capital criminal case, which is now the next stop in this hearing. A request for your client's mental evaluation should have happened months ago. The state is obligated to do that due to the severity of the crime. However, the defense should be seeking their own evaluation of the defendant's mental state."

In another rare move, the JP said, "I appointed you because you have a good record before the court, but not in a case of this magnitude. I am concerned for the defendant's sake that you are not prepared to take this to the level where it is going, jeopardizing the representation of the accused. A litany of appeals will certainly follow. Therefore, something I have never done before, and never thought I would, is to suggest that you resign from this case. I am going to leave it up to you, but that is my strong suggestion.

"I wanted you to hear this," he said to the prosecutor, "because if counsel takes my advice and resigns, the court will have to appoint a new defense attorney. That will prolong this case moving to a capital trial, while the new attorney familiarizes himself/herself on the charges and the evidence."

Neither the prosecuting attorney, nor the defense attorney said anything. They both sat in silence. The JP said he would like to have an answer in the next 48 hours, then excused both attorneys.

When District Attorney Gould initially received notice from the LVPD about the arrest and charges brought against the defendant, he requested several staff members to attend a briefing. The preliminary data indicated that a horrific crime had been committed; two lives were lost and there's no way to know how many more lives might be negatively impacted by these killings. He assigned his assistant, Edna Lingreen, to be the lead prosecutor on the case. He told his staff that the crimes warranted capital punishment in the state of Nevada. The DA also knew that his assistant, Lingreen, did not whole-heartedly support the death penalty. She did not oppose capital punishment. The Assistant DA simply did not endorse the execution believing it to be carried out in less than humane ways.

Death by lethal injection became established nationwide as the most common form of execution. Most states determined lethal injection to be more humane than death by cyanide gas, introduced as a means of execution in the 1920's. Cyanide replaced electrocution, introduced as early as the 1890's. Both of those types left a trail of gruesome failures in the execution process. Now there were reports that lethal injection may have more botched results than other methods. The cocktail mixtures of the lethal drugs sometimes failed and the accused died slowly and in agony. That's not the norm, but it did happen too frequently and Lingreen did not like the pain and suffering that the accused would go through. Even though it was probably far more humane than the way their victims were killed.

The DA knew that a court trial would require his office to have an 'all hands-on deck' approach. Unanimity on the team would be important. The evidence presented, so far, convinced the DA that the crime perpetrated on the two innocent victims rose to a high level of being malicious, intentional, and evil. The defendant's criminal history covered nearly 25 years of a continuous and escalating criminal activity. His most recent criminal act, prior to this one, netted him 5 years in an Oregon prison for armed robbery. His crimes continued to worsen in violence throughout his life. Rehabilitation did not take root at any of the defendants stops along his criminal career. No remorse for his crimes convinced the DA that the accused, if given the chance, would kill again. The prosecution team and the DA's view of the crimes were aligned and they concurred that capital punishment would be the recommended penalty. The DA's administrative team also explored the possibility that the defense would invoke an insanity plea on behalf of the accused.

CHAPTER THIRTY-ONE

Trial Delayed

Nearly a week passed since the unusual discussion in the JP chambers. The Assistant DA, Lingreen, notified Tom Malloy of the most recent issue at the close of the 2nd preliminary hearing. Lingreen told Tom that the current defense counsel resigned at the request of the JP. A new one would be appointed soon. The trial would be delayed once a new attorney gets appointed, so that person can review the case and be adequately prepared for trial. The JP said the trial could be scheduled for October, but that now looks highly doubtful. The JP upheld the 'no bail' status for the defendant, recognizing him as a flight risk. She told Tom that her office will be recommending the death penalty for the two murders. A different judge will be assigned to the case, since it now becomes a capital murder trial.

Tom asked if the accused finally admitted to the crimes.

"No," said Lingreen. "He continues to deny any involvement in the murders. His former defense attorney tried to lay the groundwork that there are no witnesses, and that we have not provided a motive for the crime. I am certain the new defense council will appeal the 'no bail' decision, but I don't think that will get very far. The defendant is notably a high-risk individual and he will flee if given a chance. The evidence is quite convincing that this guy committed the murders, and we will hold him accountable."

"What's next?" asked Tom.

"The new judge appointed to the case will likely be the one appointing new counsel for the defense. After he does that, he will hold one, maybe two, conferences to make sure the new attorneys are making reasonable progress enabling the judge to set a trial date. I will let you know if there are any changes to what we have just talked about," said Lingreen. "By the way, how are you and your family doing through all of this?"

"I would like to tell you that we are doing fine, but we are not. I closed my dry-cleaning business. Inez and I started that business shortly after we moved to California. I could not muster the will to open the doors every day without her being there. My in-laws converted my detached garage into a studio apartment. I have moved out of the house that my wife and I first moved into when we came to California. I am living in the converted garage at the back of the house, and renting out the larger house, our home of many years. This has helped to supplement my income, since I closed the dry-cleaning business.

"My daughter, Margie, who you have met and talked to, has been a lot of help. I know she misses her mom and sister as much as I do. You probably know that the LVPD cleared Gaynard of any connection involving the killer.

"My daughter, Norma, purchased a life insurance policy that has a double indemnity clause for accidental death. This was no accident, but her husband, Gaynard, received $20,000 from the insurance company. Margie has not talked to Gaynard since the murders. She is of the opinion that he is responsible for what happened to Inez and Norma. I don't know if that will ever change. Life doesn't go on for everyone, Margie is getting through this the best she can. For me, this seems to have become a perpetual nightmare."

"Mr. Malloy," said Lingreen, "I'm sorry to hear that. This type of tragedy takes a toll on people that we can't imagine. It really is unfair."

"Well," said Tom, "let me know when the legal wrangling gets solved and when this will go to court."

"Yes, I will," she said.

Chief Justice David Zenoff appointed Judge Thomas Novickas to the case. Judge Novickas served on the judicial bench for nearly ten years. Just about everyone in the legal field knew Judge Novickas to be an avid hiker and a lifetime baseball fan. He displayed autographed photos in his office of Ernie Banks, Ron Santo and pitcher Dick Drott. He never abandoned his favorite team: the Chicago Cubs. The judge also displayed a very distinguishable feature; a gold left cuspid tooth. Sometimes noticeable when he spoke. Always noticeable when he smiled.

Judge Novickas appointed two new defense attorneys for the accused: Mike Wright and Steve McGinnis. He informed both of them that the defendant did not want to be represented, that he wanted to defend himself in a criminal trial.

Working diligently to catch up on the proceedings, it still took nearly 5 more months for the newly appointed defense attorneys to familiarize themselves with the case and to initiate a mental health evaluation of their client. Surprisingly, the new defense team threw yet another wrinkle into the legal process.

CHAPTER THIRTY-TWO

A Darker Plan

A trial date was still pending, eleven months after the murders.
One Saturday afternoon, during a family barbeque at Tom's house in San Gabriel, Tom shared a decision he made. He sat down in a lawn chair next to a couple of his nephews: Ron and Curt.

Tom said, "How are you two doing? I'm sorry I haven't been able to get to any of your games this past year. I don't think I missed any of your little league games when you were both younger. Now, you're both in high school, almost grown up."

"We understand," Curt replied.

"I wish I did," said Tom. "This murder trial is wearing on me. Not knowing what happened, or why, is not making it any better. The church tells me to forgive those that trespass against you. That hasn't been easy to do. This has taken my heart and soul from me. I don't know if I could find forgiveness, even if the suspected killer asked for it. How do you forgive someone if they don't want to be forgiven? If they deny they have done anything wrong to harm you, what's the point? It won't bring Norma and Inez back, and I doubt it will give me any peace.

"Father Brown told me that life can be very difficult. We will be faced with unforeseeable hardships. I could never have imagined this."

After a period of silence between Tom and his nephews, Tom said, "I've decided to go to the rectory at the church. I'm going to borrow a priest's robe.

I know my way around there rather well. I don't expect anyone to ask me any questions about why I'm there, or what I'm doing. Then I will go to the Nevada prison, where they are holding the alleged killer, and ask to see him. I will be wearing a priest's robe when I enter the visitor check-in area at the prison.

"I'll tell the guards at the check-in desk that the prisoner has asked to see a priest. That's a rather common request of a prisoner. I'm sure they will let me in and take me to his cell. I don't expect many, if any, questions from the guards. Priests visit prisoners all the time for confession, and for the prisoners to cleanse their souls. I want to see this guy up close; I want to peer into his eyes, and ask him if he killed Inez and Norma. I will know by the look in his eyes if he did it. If I am convinced that he killed them, I will have a gun concealed under the robe, I'll pull it out and shoot him."

Temporarily stunned by Tom's plan, Ron said, "You would not make it out of there, you would be arrested. Then what?"

"My will is all but gone. I am wasting away, I might as well waste away in prison. The police arrested someone they believe committed the murders, but it's been almost a year, and nothing has come of it. I need to know if he did it," said Tom.

His nephews were silent, contemplating what Tom just told them, then Ron said, "Tom, have you thought this through? The part I don't like is that if you do this, then we lose you, too. There is not one of us here today that does not feel the same way: angry, sad, heartbroken. That would be compounded if you were also taken from our lives. I get it, I know how you feel, and none of us would blame you. The law might, but we won't. Still, we don't want to lose you."

Tom did not respond, his gaze did not fall upon his nephews. He lit a cigarette, stood up and slowly walked away.

Curt said, "Wow, do you think he will go through with that?"

"I doubt it," said Ron.

"I'm not sure, I would not be too surprised if he did," said Curt.

His nephews sat and reminisced about their uncle going to the baseball games. They both played at the Bassett Little League Field, and now at the Pony-Colt field. Tom would drive about ten miles each way to watch the games.

"I remember him walking up and down the fence line from home plate to the outfield. He never made a comment, or shouted out any instructions from the sidelines. But he sure made his presence known by all of his pacing. Even after the games, he never made a comment about an error or an out. He would always talk about the great plays and hits that we made," said Curt.

Ron laughed and said, "He always found the silver lining in the dark cloud, even after an obviously bad game."

Tom loved sports, that probably carried over from his boxing prowess. His nephews also noticed how Tom missed more and more of their games. Since the murders, he noticeably slowed down and appeared to take less interest about life in general. His pacing of the sidelines had all but stopped. He mostly stood outside the fence line at first base, or third base, fingers laced into the chain-link, and just watched the game. They noticed how subtly he became less energetic and frailer. Lately he did not attend the ball games at all. His nephews talked a while longer, concurring that they hope he does not act on his plan, that would be heaping tragedy upon tragedy.

Then Ron said, "I feel bad for Tom. The one person that could probably help get through this is Mitchell. He hasn't been around since the funeral."

Curt moved his head from left to right and back again scanning the scene of people. He said, "That's Mitchell's choice, I think it is a poor one, but there's not much that can be done about it. Good thing Tom has Margie, she seems to be holding up alright."

"I heard that Gaynard has been drinking quite a bit since the murders. I'm sure he's come to the realization that his actions caused both Inez and Norma to be killed. There's still a lot of ill feelings toward him," said Ron.

"I, for one, don't want to be in his company. If I think about him, or hear his name, I think about losing Norma and Inez. He committed a pretty selfish act. It still angers me."

"Me too, I don't have anything good to say about him."

The two of them sat without saying anything for a few moments, then Ron said, "I sure miss Norma. I remember when my folks first moved to California. I was five years old and did not know anyone. Norma wanted to make sure that there were plenty of friends to keep me occupied. The two of us went around the neighborhood and she introduced me to all the kids my age. They all knew her and I always looked forward to visiting. I still remem-ber most of them: Kelly, Jim, George, Bob, Connie, Dianne. They have all moved away from here, I've often wonder what they are doing. One of them owned a dog, a Labrador, I can't remember the dog's name: Smokey, maybe? The dog always ran around the neighborhood with us. We were like the Little Rascals. Norma would give the dog treats whenever it came around. Yeah, I'll probably miss her the rest of my life."

Curt nodded, affirming he felt the same way about missing his older cousin. "Remember when she would put us in the trunk of her car and sneak us into the drive-in movie?" Glancing across the back yard, he said, "Heads up, here comes the Bluebird."

Bluebird is a nickname given to their younger cousin, Isla Perry. Her Grandpa gave her that nickname right after she was born. He said she had the prettiest blue eyes he's ever seen.

Isla came running through the crowd of people. She told her older cousins, "Mom said we can go to the park, but only if you take us."

"She did?" said Curt, "Well, it looks like our afternoon has been cut out for us."

Glancing back at Isla he said, "Go get the rest of your troops and let's go."

Ron said chuckling, "That kid has more energy than all of us put together. I am going to ask Tom if he wants to join us, I doubt that he will, but I'll make the offer."

CHAPTER THIRTY-THREE

Defense: Exonerate the Accused

Two weeks later. Tom received a call from the Clark County DA's office. He learned that the newly appointed judge to the case notified the defense that a trial date will be set as soon as the defense confirms that they are prepared to go to trial.

Tom felt relieved to hear this current news, hopeful there would be an ending to this fiasco. *It's coming up on a year since my wife and daughter were murdered, I can't help but thinking there will be many more delays.*

Shortly after the DA's office informed Tom of the pending trial date, the defense lawyers contacted the judge. They introduced a request that surprised Judge Novickas. The trial date would be pushed back several months, so the new attorneys could familiarize themselves with the case. Now the defense sent a letter to the judge requesting that he review all civil matters that are currently scheduled before the courts. In their letter, they reminded the judge that their client has been charged for a capital criminal offense, and capital offenses takes priority over all civil litigation. They requested any, and all, civil cases be rescheduled and the murder trial be moved to the front of the court schedule as allowed by law. They requested that the trial proceed barring all further delays. Their client is innocent, and he wants to clear his name, and be released from incarceration. They also requested that the accused be released on his own recognizance.

The judge called the opposing attorneys to a meeting. He said, "I have read the request by the defense, reviewed all current and pending court cases, and I am prepared to move up the trial date. However, I do not want the DA's office to be blindsided by this unusual request. So, let me ask you, Ms. Lingreen, are you prepared to proceed in this trial, if I set the trial date to begin on May 3rd?"

"Your Honor," said Ms. Lingreen, "My office has been prepared to present our case for the past year, we have no objections to you setting the trial date for early May."

"So be it," said the judge. "The trial will begin six weeks from today. Jury selection will begin in the next 4 weeks."

CHAPTER THIRTY-FOUR

Graphic Photos Omitted

Jury selection started on time four weeks later. The judge began the process by asking the prospective jurors about their legal qualifications to serve on a jury. There were 43 people in the jury pool that first day. The opposing legal teams were allowed to question any or all of them before they made a recommendation to keep or dismiss the juror. Several potential jurors were excused for an actual or implied bias: a challenge for cause. The attorney from either side can request that the court remove the individual juror under this category. In addition to the phase of the jury selection, the judge gave both sides six peremptory challenges. This allowed the attorneys to remove up to six potential jurors for no stated reason. On the fourth day of the selection process, the jury pool managed to be whittled down to 12 jurors. The judge confirmed those 12 and two alternate jurors.

One week before the trial began, Assistant District Attorney Lingreen, contacted Tom Malloy. She told him that by all appearances, the trial would begin next week. She asked Tom if he, or any of his family members were going to be at the trial.

"Margie and I have been talking about it, neither one of us want to relive the details of the murders. Personally, I relive that horrible tragedy every day. But I want to see the person that did this awful thing. So, we are planning to be there for the start of the trial. I don't think we will be there for its entirety. Some of Inez's siblings and other relatives have expressed that they too want to be there when the trial starts. They said they can't get time off of work to be there for the whole trial. Norma's husband, Gaynard, implied that he's planning to be there also. He's not doing well, and we have not seen or heard from him for several months. I will contact him regarding this latest information. Drinking has gotten the better of him since the murders. My son, Mitchell, can't decide if he wants to go, or not. So, I'm not sure who all will be there from the family, could be eight or ten people that might show up."

"OK Tom. I'll make sure that the row of seats directly behind where I'll be sitting is reserved for you and your family members," said Lingreen.

Just a few days prior to the start of the trial, the defense attorney requested a meeting with the assistant DA. They met at the DA's office.

"This is your meeting, tell me what's on your mind," said Lingreen.

I have a list of items that I want removed from being shown or used as evidence in the courtroom," said defense attorney Wright.

Lingreen did not respond but waited for Wright to share his list of requests.

"First of all, I do not want the jury to be shown the close-up photos of the victim's head shot wounds. We are willing to admit that the victims were both shot in the head at close range. I will not agree, or suggest, that my client shot the victims."

"I also want to have the FBI people removed from your expert witness list. They were not part of the initial investigation or on-site evaluation. They should not be able to testify or submit written summary. You also have on your list two people from Portland, Oregon that were allegedly robbed at gunpoint by my client, they too should not be allowed to testify. I also want capital punishment removed as a recommendation and that my client be remanded to the state mental hospital."

"Mr. Wright," interrupted Lingreen. "I appreciate you contacting me about your requests. However, you should know that I will not remove any of the expert witnesses from testifying. Regarding the death penalty recommendation, this office wrestled with that decision. I personally am not a proponent of the death penalty. But these crimes were so heinous, so gruesome, and your client has all the propensity to do this again if set free on the streets. The answer to your requests is one that you don't want to hear. The answer is no, I will not change anything in this trial going forward. I am leaning toward not showing the photos of the victim's head shot wounds. Although, those photos are powerful tools when shown to the jury. I can spare the jury and the victims' family of having to see the damage caused by the gunshots. I will have the expert witnesses go into great detail on graphic explanation to the jury about what happened as a result of those gunshot wounds. The Clark County M.E. is prepared to report to the jury the findings of the autopsy, gunshot, bruising, lacerations, and rape. *IF*, and this is a big if, I agree to not show the close-up photos of the head wounds, I will be showing a litany of crime scene photos. And, by all means, I intend to put the FBI agents on the witness stand to describe in painstaking detail their review of the findings. Now, Mr. Wright, if I agree to not show those close-up photos, you will agree to confirm the cause of death?"

"Yes, we will agree to the cause of death: gunshot to the head of both victims. We will not agree that our client is guilty of those crimes. I am sure that you know I can file a brief to the judge asking him to not allow the other items that we talked about."

"My answer is still no. You can certainly file a brief with the judge but I would not put much credence on that effort. Your client committed a horrific crime and the state will use all the evidence at its disposal to prove your client committed the act, and did so out of malice and showing no regard for human life."

By agreeing to acknowledge how the victims were killed, the prosecution agreed not to show the close-up photos of the victims faces and head wounds to the jury. The on-scene forensic team and the Medical Examiner took explicit photos detailing the impact of the bullets, and damage, to the victims' heads. The photos were horrific, and the defense believed the photos would taint the jury's perception of their client. All other photos of the death scene would be allowed. The Assistant DA agreed to the stipulation, but made it clear to the defense that the wounds caused by the gun shots to the head would be described in verbal detail by her expert witnesses without showing the photos.

CHAPTER THIRTY-FIVE

Trial Drama

On May 3rd, Judge Novickas called the court to order at 9:05 a.m., and the trial began in the case of the State of Nevada vs. Roy Warren Osborn. The judge glanced around at the nearly full courtroom. Several college age people were seated. The media also doggedly followed the trial process. One of the law professors at the state university excused his senior class students to attend the trial. He told them that they may never defend or prosecute a case like this. But if they should, watching the whole debate unfold before them would be an invaluable lesson.

The judge asked the prosecution to make their opening remarks.

Assistant DA, Lingreen, approached the jury and said, "Ladies and gentlemen of the jury, you are about to hear the gruesome details of a double homicide. I want to apologize to you in advance of having to put you through this. The defendant," she turned and pointed at Osborn, "has committed one of the most horrific killings in Clark County. Two beautiful women lost their lives." She took a few steps backwards to the large photos of the two women displayed on the easels. The photos were the same ones that were shown at the funeral. She moved her right hand slowly toward the photos drawing the attention of the jurors to the two victims.

Then she continued in her opening statement. "A husband and father lost his wife and daughter. Lots and lots of the victims' relatives are still trying to put their lives back together while trying to understand the devastating loss of two people they counted on and loved very much. Nothing we do in the courtroom can bring them back. But what you can do, is provide justice for the victims and their family. The people will demonstrate during the course of this trial that the defendant, Roy Warren Osborn, saw an opportunity to rob, kidnap and harm, two innocent women on the night of March 27, over 13 months ago.

"The victims arrived in town that afternoon accompanied by the in-laws of the younger victim, Norma Widick. They came to Las Vegas to retrieve an abandoned pick-up truck that belonged to Mrs. Widick's husband, Gaynard Widick. One week prior to the murders, Norma Widick reported her husband missing from their Alhambra, California residence. The in-laws drove the pick-up truck back to Alhambra that afternoon. Inez Malloy and Norma Widick, mother and daughter, chose to stay in Las Vegas overnight and drive home the following day. But they never made it home. They never made it back to their hotel room that fateful night.

"On that fateful night at approximately 11:30 p.m., the defendant hid in the back seat floor-board area of Mrs. Widick's 1957 Chevrolet. The two women experienced car trouble when they arrived at the hotel/casino several hours earlier. The key to the trunk of the vehicle broke off and they needed to locate a lock smith to make repairs.

"Their personal belongings were in the trunk of the car. The hotel concierge found a locksmith that would stay open after hours and wait for the two women to bring their car to the locksmith shop. After the car trunk key was removed and the lock replaced, the two women exited the repair shop parking lot in Norma's '57 Chevy.

"The defendant hid on the back seat floorboard of the car while the mother and daughter paid for the repairs in the locksmith office. They could not see into the back seat due to the darkness of the night, especially onto the floor of the vehicle. As Inez began to drive the car out of the parking lot, the defendant rose up from the back seat area, pointed a gun at Inez Malloy.

"He grabbed a handful of her hair and pulled it tight, not allowing her to move her head. He ordered her to drive the car out of town.

"Several miles later, he ordered Mrs. Malloy to turn onto Blue Diamond Road. A desolate road about five miles outside the city limits. He hit Inez

Malloy several times knocking her unconscious then brutally raped the younger victim: Norma Widick. He then shot both women in the back of the head at point blank range, killing both of them instantly.

"The nearest residence to the murder scene was approximately one mile away. No one could hear the gun shot, the screaming, or the voices of the victims or the accused. He went through both of their purses taking what money he could find.

"He pulled both victims out of the vehicle and left them lying on the edge of the asphalt road. In his haste to leave the crime scene, he ran over both victims as he fled.

"The defendant returned to Las Vegas and parked the car in a lot of a hotel in the downtown area. The lot attendant noticed a broken window, stains on the front seat, a gun, and a stained shirt in the back seat. He notified hotel security, who then notified the police.

"The police staked out the parking lot, waiting for the driver to return to the car. The defendant returned to claim that vehicle approximately two hours after parking it. The LVPD initially held him on charges of auto theft because he could not prove ownership of the vehicle. He claimed, at the time of his arrest, the vehicle belonged to his girlfriend. Murder, robbery, kidnapping, and rape were added to the auto theft charges shortly after his arrest.

"We will bring in experts from the Clark County Sheriff's Department, the Clark County Medical Examiner, a ballistics expert and blood analysis expert from the Federal Bureau of Investigation. We will also recreate the death scene for evidence gathered by the LVPD forensic team. Two expert gun witnesses will testify on the weapon used in the killings. At the end of the trial you, the jury, will have enough evidence to convict the defendant on two counts of murder in the first degree, auto theft, kidnapping, rape and robbery.

"We will not be showing you close up photos of the victims' heads by an earlier agreement between opposing counsels. However, you will get a detailed explanation of the horrific damage caused by the gunshot wounds. The final horrifying minutes of the victims' lives will be reviewed with you, leaving no doubt in your minds as to the atrocious and shocking crimes the defendant committed against these two women." Lingreen paused and then thanked the jurors, then walked back to the prosecutor's table and sat down.

The defendant acquiesced on his position to defend himself and sat silently between the two court appointed attorneys. Defense Attorney Wright stood and walked over to the jury box.

"The Assistant DA would like for you to believe my client is guilty of this heinous crime. This is a very weak case, and at its conclusion, you will agree with me that my client should have never been charged. Nonetheless, this case has been brought before you, the jury.

"I would like to have you focus on a couple of key issues throughout this trial. First of all, the prosecution does not have a motive for the crime, and they will not provide one to you. Secondly, the prosecution has not provided any eye witnesses to the crime, only circumstantial evidence that does not tie my client to the murders.

"The defendant came to Las Vegas looking for work. He is an unemployed welder. The prosecution must prove to you that there is absolutely no doubt that the defendant committed the crimes for which these unfounded charges have been brought against him. You will easily be able to determine that there is a mountain of doubt in the prosecutor's case. I expect a not guilty verdict, and the defendant to be acquitted on all charges brought forth by the prosecution. Thank you." Defense Attorney Wright looked at each of the jurors then walked back to his table and sat down.

The judge then asked the Assistant DA, Lingreen, if she would like to call her first witness.

Before she could answer, the defense attorney stood abruptly, and somewhat noisily, as the wooden chair legs scraped on the tile floor as the chair scooted backwards.

He said, "Your Honor, my client would like to enter a plea of insanity at the time of the murders. He is left without an alternative to do so since the Assistant DA has announced she will be seeking the death penalty. The state of Nevada prohibits the death penalty conviction on the grounds of insanity, or mental instability. As I just said to the jury, I expect a not guilty verdict, but if the jury convicts on what I deem as only circumstantial evidence, then my client should not, and cannot, face the death penalty on those findings, which we would appeal anyway should that occur. I am requesting that the trial be postponed until such time that a full mental health analysis of my client can be completed."

The judge asked Lingreen if she would like to respond to this latest request.

She rose from her chair, "Your Honor, we anticipated and expected this move from the defense counsel. I am surprised that they waited until the start of the trial to raise the concern of their client's mental state. I expected them to do that when I announced we would seek the death penalty over six months ago.

"I do not see any reason to delay the trial to a further date, especially since the defense, and the defendant, quoted state law to bring this trial forward to an earlier hearing date.

"The glaring problem about the request of the defense is that there is no way to determine the state of mind of the defendant at the time of the slayings, which occurred over a year ago. The court is obligated to allow an insanity plea and for the defense to seek supporting psychological analysis. Allow me to suggest that we do not delay this trial any further, but allow it to move forward simultaneously during the psychological analysis. As I stated to the jury in my opening comments, the defendant knew what he wanted to do, planned it, got caught and lied about everything that tied him to the crimes. I fully anticipate a guilty verdict.

"This request by the defense would create a delay to the court's decision on the penalty of the verdict. That would only happen in the event that the mental review of the defendant goes longer than the trial. If that were to happen, then you, Your Honor, would be required to delay the penalty phase of the trial until such time that you have reviewed the findings of the defendants' mental capacity.

"Again, Your Honor, I anticipate a guilty verdict on two counts of first-degree murder. A review of the defendant's mental state will prove that he is fit to stand trial for all the crimes of which he is accused. Therefore, I have no objections to the request, only that the mental evaluation and trial run simultaneously so there are no further delays for the victims and their loved ones."

The judge said, "I will consider that the psychological profile be conducted simultaneously with the trial, there have been enough delays already. Counsel for the defense, do you concur?"

"No, Your Honor, I do not. I request that the mental evaluation of my client be conducted ahead of the trial moving forward. I also request that my client be housed in a state mental hospital during the course of the trial and his mental evaluation," replied Attorney Wright as he stood waiting for the judge to rule on the objection.

"Your client is here for a capital crime. If you, the defense, failed to request a mental evaluation, the court would be obligated to do so for his own protection. His guilt, or innocence, is not predicated on his mental state: he did it, or he did not do it. The jury can determine a verdict, based on the evidence presented to them. If there is a guilty verdict, then sentencing will come after the jury deliberations. A mental health evaluation should, and can occur, long before the jury enters those deliberations," said the judge.

The defense started to protest, but the judge raised his hand to stop any comments and said, "I can find no reason to send your client to a state hospital at this time. I reviewed all the preliminary hearing notes and found that District Judge Zenoff also spoke to the defendant prior to the prelim. In his notes he mentions that in his opinion, the defendant is of sound mind and capable of proceeding on to the trial. We all know that most of us presiding on the bench do not claim to be the ones rendering a person's state of mind. State law allows and requires that to be done by recognized mental health professionals. The trial mental health analysis will proceed concurrently.

"The defense and the prosecution will conduct independent reviews and bring whomever they choose to meet the defendant and conduct their respective reviews of his mental state. I am sure, as you have stated, this is not a surprise to either one of you, and you already have evaluators in the wings waiting to get started. I will be calling upon each of you next week for an update on your progress. Now, is the prosecution ready to call their first witness?"

CHAPTER THIRTY-SIX

The Weapon

David Visser, a gun collector, took the stand first for the prosecution. David stood about 6 feet tall, weighing around 190 pounds. He sported near shoulder length sandy-blonde hair, a moustache and close-trimmed beard. He wore slacks, a long sleeve shirt, no tie. She introduced him as a gun collector, buyer and seller from the Portland, Oregon area.

"Mr. Visser," said Lingreen," would you tell the court your background, specifically regarding handguns."

"My wife, Kathy, and I have collected hand guns for several decades. Our passion is in the more historical handguns, from the early western days dating from the American Revolution to the late 1890's. We also buy and sell hand guns that were more recently made."

"Can you identify this handgun?" The prosecutor picked up a gun laying on a table, a tag on the gun said: Exhibit 1.

"Yes, that's a Colt manufactured .38 caliber revolver," said Visser nodding.

The defense objected, stating that the gun, and type, were already established in discovery.

Lingreen said, "Your Honor, I am only trying to establish the defendant's familiarity with this type of handgun, if I can proceed."

The judge allowed her to continue.

The prosecutor then rolled another table into the courtroom. A large, pale-blue blanket covered the items on the table. She pulled back the blanket to reveal 10 different handguns. She asked Visser if he has ever seen the guns on the table before. He shook his head and said no. The prosecutor picked up one of the guns, placed it in her open hands for the jury and the witness to see. She then asked Visser to identify the weapon, but did not hand it to him. She kept the gun displayed in her open hands. The prosecutor displayed each of the guns on the table. Visser identified all of them and did not handle the guns, or leave the witness chair.

"Thank you," said Lingreen. "Your Honor, I wanted to establish the expert background of the witness. These guns were borrowed from the LVPD evidence room. They are all tagged identifying make, model, and manufacturer. The witness correctly identified every one of them."

The defense objected by stating that the prosecution resorted to theatrics and it has no part in the criminal trial.

The judge weighed the objection then said he would allow the prosecutor a few more questions to establish the credibility of the witness.

"Now, Mr. Visser, have you ever seen the defendant before this trial?" asked Lingreen.

"Yes, I certainly have. He robbed my wife and I at gun point in Portland, Oregon about six years ago."

The defense attorney objected again, saying the defendant is not on trial for what might have happened in Portland, Oregon six years ago.

Lingreen responded by stating she is establishing the defendant's familiarity regarding the gun used in the slayings.

The judge overruled the objection and allowed the questioning to continue.

"Tell the court about your encounter involving the defendant," said the prosecutor.

"It was around 10:00 p.m. on a Saturday night. We just finished up at a gun show at the Portland Fair Grounds. We were loading our inventory into our van. The defendant appeared out of the dark. He walked up behind my wife, grabbed her around the neck using his left arm and pointed the gun at her head holding the gun in his right hand. He demanded our money. We were carrying just over $800 in cash, we gave it to him. He took it, pushed my wife to the ground, and ran off into the dark."

"What happened next?"

"We went back inside the building and called the police. We were able to give the police a better description of the weapon than of the robber. The robber wore a heavy coat and a baseball cap. I focused more on the gun than on his face.

"Later that same night, the police notified us that they arrested a suspect and wanted us to come to the station. When we arrived, they showed us the gun they confiscated from the suspect, a Colt .38 caliber revolver. They also found $835 in cash on the man they arrested, a baseball cap and heavy coat. I confirmed that the gun they showed to be the same gun used to rob us at the fairgrounds."

The defense objected to the fact that the witness stated the time to be after 10:00 p.m. Making it too dark to get a good look at the robber.

"Your Honor," said Lingreen, "I am establishing that the witness described the weapon to the Portland Police, the same weapon used in the robbery, validating his expertise on hand gun identification."

"Continue," said the judge.

"Mr. Visser, is this the same gun used to rob you and your wife in Portland, Oregon?" she picked up the gun tagged as evidence and showed it to the witness.

Mr. Visser said, "No, this is not the same gun. There are subtle differences in just about every gun. The trained eye will notice the shade of the bluing on the barrel. Sometimes the gun owner will change the grips of the gun creating a different appearance. The grips on this gun are different from the one used to rob my wife and I. It is the same make, same model; a Colt .38 caliber revolver."

"Is this style of hand gun easy to get?" asked Lingreen.

"It is not the most popular, but it is less expensive than other hand guns. Most people prefer a semi-automatic. A gun that takes a magazine in the handle and holds upwards of nine rounds per magazine. The magazine is easily ejected and another magazine can go into the gun handle quickly. The shell casings eject after each shot, so there is very little time wasted in reloading.

"When a revolver is fired, the shell casings are not discharged, they have to be physically removed and another bullet has to be installed in each of the six holes in the cylinder of the gun. A lot more time is required to reload the revolver. The revolver is a little heavier than the semi-automatic. The lower cost of the revolver makes it an attractive purchase, but it is no less effective than the semi-automatic."

"You stated that the revolver type of a handgun, when fired, the casing of the bullet remains in the chamber of the weapon. It has to be physically removed and replaced, is that correct?

"Yes," said Visser.

"Once the gun is discharged, and the bullet leaves the chamber, can the bullet and bullet casing that remains in the revolver be matched up? This would also depend on the recovery of the spent bullet, but can the bullet, the casing and the gun be matched eliminating any doubt that the bullet came from the gun in question?"

"Absolutely," said Visser. "Ballistic testing will match up the lines of the bullet and the lines in the barrel of the gun. The shell casings are also matched to the spent bullet. All of which can be traced back to the manufacturer. Higher power magnifying lenses are used to do this, it is a scientific analysis leaving no doubt as to the origin of the bullet, and the gun that it came from."

"Mr. Visser, is the man that robbed you and your wife at gun point in this courtroom?"

Before Visser could answer, the defense objected again. Lingreen did not wait for the judge to respond. She withdrew her question, looked at her witness and thanked him for his testimony. She said there would be no more questions.

In cross examination, the defense attorney asked Visser, "Are you now, or have you ever been in law enforcement?"

"No, to both of your questions," he said.

"Did you go to any school, or trade school to learn about guns and gun identification?" asked the defense.

"No, I served in the United States Air Force for six years, where I received extensive training on different types of firearms. Guns have always been a hobby, or a passion of mine," said Visser.

"No more questions," said the defense attorney.

The rest of the trial saw the same response from the defense toward the witnesses that the prosecutor summoned to the stand. The defense objected to most of the questions, and then would try to discredit the expertise of the witnesses. Objections by the defense were raised on nearly every question, and every response, given in testimony. The defense would also object to every piece of evidence presented by the Assistant DA throughout the trial. Their strategy, paralleling the strategy in the preliminary hearing, would be to raise a level of doubt in the jury's mind as to the accuracy of testimony, and the credibility of the DA's expert witnesses.

The witnesses brought to the stand were seated, examined, and cross examined, for an average of four hours per person. Some were on the stand longer. Constant objections and challenges can throw the prosecution off of their game plan by disrupting their delivery of pertinent information. Rattle the prosecutor, find a weakness, and exploit the weakness in the eyes of the jury is a formidable approach. Hammering away all day on every point the prosecution brings to the court would find its way into the jury deliberations. The defense reasoned that this makes it extremely difficult to convict without reasonable doubt.

Assistant DA, Lingreen, read every statement provided by the LVPD and Clark County Sheriff's office regarding the arrest of the defendant. She conducted every deposition, and studied the time line of the murders in great detail. The Assistant DA, and the DA's office believed there to be no doubt as to the guilt of the defendant. They believed he planned to do harm to the victims, beyond robbery. Every objection raised by the defense would be countered by further detailed review, and explanation, from the prosecutor, as well as the expert witnesses. She understood the strategy being employed by the defense, and seized every opportunity to eliminate reasonable doubt. Lingreen prepared for the trial, and she knew that a capital case like this one would be high profile due to the nature of the killings.

CHAPTER THIRTY-SEVEN

I Want to See His Eyes

Tom Malloy and Margie observed the proceedings in the courthouse the entire week. They spoke to Lingreen every day. During the trial, Tom kept a steady gaze on the defendant. At one point, Defense Attorney Wright turned in his chair and noticed Tom staring intently at his client. Osborn's attorney turned back in his chair and mumbled a few words to his client. Defendant Osborn did not glance over at Tom, but remained stoic, looking only at his note pad and the witness stand.

The accused showed little to no reaction from the comments by the expert witnesses. He showed no indication of emotion or remorse. Tom saw the accused display only an attitude of indifference and arrogance to the proceedings. He watched how the defendant reacted to the incriminating evidence brought against him. On a few occasions Tom watched the accused turn to speak to his attorney during witness testimony. He also saw him writing and passing notes to his attorney, sometimes moving his pen vigorously over the paper.

I just want to look this guy in the eye. Tom learned to read a man's eyes as an amateur boxer. He could see fear, defeat, confidence, but most of all, he could tell what his opponent would do next by looking into his eyes. He knew that if given the opportunity, for only a moment, to stare into the accused killer's eyes, he would know instantly as to his guilt or innocence.

At one point during the trial, Tom leaned forward from his seat and placed his left hand on the railing between the court spectators and the legal counsel. It appeared that he may attempt to bound over the railing to get to the defendant. The bailiff saw this and walked in front of Tom. He asked him to remove his hand from the railing and sit back in his seat. Tom did not look at the bailiff, his eyes were focused on the defendant. Margie reached out and put her hand on her dad's forearm and quietly said, "Please do as he asks, sit back." The incident lasted only a few brief moments. Then the bailiff turned toward the judge and gave a slight nod of his head indicating everything is alright. The trial proceeded.

The defense felt thankful that the sheriff's detention center fitted Osborn in a new suit, or one that looked new. A light blue two-piece suit that fit him very well. He appeared clean shaven including a fresh haircut. By all accounts, he did not appear to be someone that could commit these awful murders.

Other than his nephews, Tom never shared his thoughts about taking a priest's robe from the church rectory and assuming the identity of a priest. Then bluff his way into the prison area to see the accused and decide for himself if he committed the crimes.

On Friday, when court recessed for the weekend, Tom told Lingreen that he and his daughter needed to return home and would not be able to attend the trial next week.

Lingreen assured them that it would be okay. "The jury saw that you were there, and they can tell what you are going through. They will think about that during their deliberations. Next week is going to be a lot rougher. I will be calling upon the forensic experts and the Medical Examiner. They will go into detailed descriptions of what happened and that is going to get a lot more graphic. I would certainly understand that you don't want to put yourself through that part. I believe whole-heartedly that this man is guilty. I must get very descriptive in my presentation to the jury, so they know and understand everything he did that night he killed your loved ones. Reconstructing that fatal night and explaining it to the jury can get a little brutal. I believe the state will be justified in issuing the death penalty. I want the jury, and the judge, to feel the same way.

"You heard the judge order a mental evaluation of the accused. I doubt that will change anything. I will let you know how things are going. If you cannot return, I will contact you as soon as the jury renders a decision. Do you have any questions of me?"

Margie spoke up immediately, "During the opening statements earlier in the week, when the defense said they were entering an insanity plea, is that an admission to the crime?"

"Not exactly," said Lingreen. "The defense team is tasked to not only trying to get their client acquitted, they are scrambling to save his life. When I declared that we would seek the death penalty, it became a priority for them to try and prevent that from happening. It will not delay a conviction by the jury, but it could delay sentencing from the judge if the evaluation goes longer than the trial. Again, I am not giving it any credence, he knew the consequences of his crime at the time of the murders, and the evidence will substantiate it."

Tom asked, "So, the defendant will continue to deny that he killed my wife and daughter, and is it the judge who ultimately decides whether he is sane, or not?"

"His denial is expected. We will prove that he did it, even if he chooses to continue to deny what he has done. Regarding his insanity plea, the judge will decide on that issue. He will confer with other district judges on the findings, and recommend a decision that will be based on reports submitted by mental health experts from both sides," said Lingreen.

"What are the chances of me getting a few minutes alone to talk to the accused?" asked Tom.

Lingreen knew that would not be possible, and did not respond to the question.

Margie glanced back and forth between her dad and the prosecutor. She did not expect that question and nervously awaited the prosecutor's answer.

After a short uncomfortable pause, Tom said, "That's what I thought. Probably not much of a chance that the victim's family can look him in the eye."

Then Assistant DA Lingreen said, "I'm sorry Tom."

They said their goodbyes and the Assistant DA said she will keep them updated on the progress of the trial.

She prepared for the trial to resume the following week by reviewing her notes for the individuals she would call to the stand on Monday morning.

Nothing she did could prepare her for what would happen in court during the upcoming week.

CHAPTER THIRTY-EIGHT

Missing Books

Monday morning, Lingreen began by calling the parking lot attendant, Don Long, to the stand. She began to establish the timeline of the murders, connecting the crime and the car to the defendant. The defense continued to object to testimony by the parking lot attendant, and to the evidence presented by the prosecution. This tactic, closely similar in many ways to that employed by the previous defense counsel during the prelim, who the JP asked to resign from the case.

Next, the arresting officer, Sergeant Schenkenberger, took the stand. "How many years have you been employed by the LVPD?"

"Twelve years," he said.

"Please tell the court about the circumstances that led to the arrest of the defendant."

Sergeant Schenkenberger began, "We received a call from the hotel security that a suspicious car recently entered and parked in the pay-to-park lot. Upon arriving, the officers observed a broken window on the passenger side of the car. They also noticed stains on the front seat of the vehicle that would later be determined to be human blood stains. They also discovered a bloody shirt in the back seat of the car, and a duffle bag. Inside the duffle bag, they found a handgun. The handgun would be determined to have been the murder weapon. The fingerprints on the gun belonged to the person we arrested. When the suspect returned to the parking lot to reclaim the vehicle, I questioned him about the car contents and legal ownership of the car. He would not give me a name to match to the registration of the vehicle. I made the decision that the suspect stole the car. We took him into custody, and booked him for auto theft at the LVPD."

The defense objected to this testimony saying, "The witness's comments should not be allowed on the grounds that the vehicle was searched illegally. The police did not have a search warrant to access the car. He did not give permission to search the vehicle. Your Honor, I would make a motion that the unlawful search and seizure of the vehicle would substantiate this being thrown out of the courts based on that fact alone, which violates my client's constitutional rights."

Judge Novickas overruled the defense motion, "The arrest of Osborn and search of the death car in a downtown parking facility did not violate his constitutional rights. I believe that to have already been established in the preliminary hearing. Your client is not the owner of the vehicle, nor could he provide any proof of ownership."

Lingreen thought that the first week of the trial moved by rather slow. Objection after objection continued to be raised by the defense in response to nearly everything said by the prosecution's expert witnesses.

Now Lingreen called Bruce Cook to the stand, the first person to discover the bodies.

The defense continually brought up the fact that the prosecution could not provide a motive to the crime. They also repeatedly pointed out that any 'eye-witness' to the crime is noticeably absent from the witness stand.

Lingreen would not take the bait that the defense counsel continued to dangle about. She viewed this only as a distraction orchestrated by the defense. The crime and all the evidence connecting the accused will provide the motive for the jury. Her list of expert witnesses and detailed forensics, she believed, would be like having a set of eyes on these two women from the moment they arrived in Las Vegas up to the time their disfigured bodies were discovered on the road side. The prosecutor laid the groundwork for the jury to choose a guilty verdict by providing mounds of physical evidence that tied the defendant to the crime, including a timeline.

When the second week of the trial began, the assistant DA called upon the first forensic specialist, Paul Mallinger, a deputy sheriff at the Clark County Sheriff's department.

"Deputy Mallinger," said Lingreen, "would you give us your full name, occupation, and how long you have been doing this work."

"I accepted the job at the Sheriff's Department just over ten years ago. I have worked in the forensic lab for most of that time. I majored in Forensics at the University of Las Vegas and minored in Criminal Law. Also, depending on my schedule, and the time of year, I give instructional assistance in science classes at the Las Vegas High School."

Deputy Mallinger answered questions on the witness stand for more than four hours. The defense objected to everything he said. When the judge broke for a recess, the defense and the defendant exited the courtroom. They went to a lockdown room where they could talk in private. The only place the defense could talk to their client outside of the actual courtroom. Due to the fact the defendant, still in custody, could not be free to roam about the building.

Upon stepping down from the witness stand, Deputy Mallinger walked past the table at which the defense sat throughout the trial. He noticed two books sitting on the table that looked familiar. The deputy went over to where the prosecutor sat and said, "Two books were stolen from me about a year ago. I think they are the very ones sitting on the defense table."

Curious, Lingreen wandered over to the defense table. She saw the two books and opened one of them. On the inside front cover, she saw the name: Paul Mallinger.

Before the prosecutor could close the book cover, and walk away, the defense attorney walked back into the courtroom to get his note pad. He saw the prosecutor at his table and noticed her gazing at one of the books. The prosecutor, in a nonchalant manner, closed the book. She kept her left hand on the book, tapping her forefinger on the cover.

The defense counsel walked up to the table, looked at Lingreen but did not say anything.

"We need to talk," she said to the defense attorney.

"Not now counselor, not now. I can assure you we will," responded Attorney Wright.

Immediately after the judge reconvened the court hearing to resume, the defense counsel stood up and said, "Your Honor, I want to file a formal complaint against the DA's office for an ethical violation of rifling through my material on the defense counsel's desk during a court recess, and during my absence."

Lingreen expressed shock and embarrassment at the accusation by the defense. It is an unwritten code, honored throughout time that the defense and prosecution work areas are out of bounds to the opposing parties. That understanding, in view of the defense, has just been breached.

Judge Novickas looked at both attorneys from his bench. He then said, "I am going to excuse the jury, and have them sequestered in the jury chambers room."

After the jury filed out of the courtroom, the judge looked at the opposing attorneys and asked attorney Wright, "Tell me what is going on here now."

Wright explained to the judge what he observed the prosecutor doing when he re-entered the courtroom to retrieve his notepad. He described it as a clear breach of ethics, stating that the prosecutor must be reprimanded for her actions and should be removed as counsel for the people.

Shifting his gaze toward the prosecutor, the judge asked, "How do you respond to the accusation that you violated defense counsel's trust?"

"Your Honor, I did not have any intentions of looking at material on the defense table. When you broke for a recess, my witness, Deputy Mallinger, approached me. He said that the two books on forensic analysis look like two books that were stolen from him. I am not accusing the defense of theft. I simply wanted to satisfy my curiosity. I opened the front cover on one of the books. The name of my witness is on the inside cover. I spoke to attorney Wright during the recess and told him that he and I need to talk. I fully expected that he could clarify how he came into possession of these books without this becoming an issue of the court and disrupting the trial."

Judge Novickas said, "Mr. Mallinger, would you please return to the witness stand, I have a few questions for you."

"Are those books on the defense table your personal property?"

"I have not examined the books. I only glanced at them as I passed by the defense table. They appear to be my personal books."

"Bailiff, would you hand the books to the deputy, so he can examine them and tell me if they are his, or not."

After looking briefly at the books, Mallinger said, "They are mine. They were taken out of my office over a year ago. I always wondered what happened to them."

"Mr. Wright, how did you come into possession of those books?" asked the judge.

"I borrowed them from the sheriff's office," said Wright. "I am often at the sheriff's office to interview clients and pick up information pertaining to a case. I saw the books and asked if I could borrow them."

"Did you borrow them for this case?" asked the judge.

"No, I did not."

"Mr. Mallinger, do the books belong to you personally, or are they property of the sheriff's office?" asked the judge.

"They are my personal books. I bought them when I attended the university. They were required for one of my science classes. I use them periodically at my job in the sheriff's department, and occasionally when I am assistant teaching at the high school."

"Mr. Wright, when did you intend to return the books to their rightful owner?" asked the judge.

"With all due respect, Your Honor, I should have returned them long ago. They were in my possession when I became the defense counsel to this case. I thought they could be useful to both me and my client."

"I have a bit of a dilemma here," said the judge. "The accusation you brought against the prosecutor includes having me remove her from this case. At a minimum, you are suggesting that she should not be arguing the case in the courtroom. That duty would then fall to someone else from her office.

"On the other hand, the prosecutor has not accused you of stealing, but you have personal property in your possession that does not belong to you. The appearance that you wrongfully came into possession of the books is apparent. The owner of that property claims the books were stolen over a year ago out of his office.

"My dilemma is that you are both challenging the integrity of each other. It is a very rare occasion when the integrity of a respected attorney is brought into question. You are both approaching a line that I do not want to see crossed. Let me make that a bit clearer; there is a line that I will not allow to be crossed in my courtroom. I believe you, Mr. Wright, that you did not steal the books, but borrowed them from someone not authorized to loan them to you.

"I also believe that Ms. Lingreen did not *rifle* through your material as you claimed. She attempted to satisfy a statement made to her by the witness. I will agree that this could have been handled differently.

"Now, this case has seen more delays and objections than is necessary. I have allowed it for the sake of the defendant, whose life and/or freedom is on trial. I have given both of you quite a bit of latitude. However, personal integrity comments by opposing counsels are beginning to surface, and I am not going to have that in my courtroom.

"Here is my ruling; I am going to deny your motion to have the prosecutor reprimanded, and removed from this case. I am going to advise her that she is to give a wide berth to the defense table and materials. I am instructing the defense to return the books to their rightful owner at the conclusion of this trial, if the owner does not want them back immediately."

"Deputy Mallinger, do you have any objections to the defense counsel using your personal books until the conclusion of this trial?" asked the judge.

"I do not," said the deputy.

The judge told the bailiff to excuse the jury from the deliberation room until tomorrow morning when the court trial would resume.

The back and forth on the issue regarding the books that began right after a noon recess, absorbed the remainder of the afternoon. Only the jury had been removed from the courtroom during the discussion on the books. All others, including the media watched the bantering, and reported on it as a major clash in the capital murder case that took up most of the afternoon.

CHAPTER THIRTY-NINE

Lab Results

The following morning, the prosecutor brought Deputy Mallinger back to the witness stand. Picking up where they left off, Lingreen asked him to tell the jury his findings on the blood types found in the murder victim's vehicle.

Deputy Mallinger: "We took samples from the blood-stained car seat, and samples found on the dashboard, steering wheel, floor carpet, and a shirt found in the back seat. We also took blood samples from both victims, as well as the defendant. We found that all the blood samples taken from the car were Type O. Both victims, mother and daughter, have Type O blood. The suspect has Type A. We did not find any Type A blood samples from the ones taken in the vehicle. The Medical Examiner found human tissue under the right-hand fingernails of the younger victim. We confirmed that the tissue belonged to that of the defendant.

"We took fingerprints from inside and outside of the car. Fingerprints were also lifted from the gun that the defendant used in the murder of the victims. We found the defendants fingerprints in multiple locations on the car; the door handle, inside and outside on the driver's side door. We found his fingerprints on the outside of the passenger door where he likely pushed the door closed from outside the car. We pulled multiple prints off the steering wheel. The only prints on the murder weapon were those of the defendant."

"Were there any other prints found on the vehicle that did not belong to the victims, or the defendant?" asked Lingreen.

"Yes, we found fingerprints on the trunk area of the car that were later determined to be that of the locksmith that worked on the car. We also found fingerprints on the outside handles and inside handles of the two back doors. Those prints we matched to the victims' in-laws that rode in the car to Las Vegas from the San Gabriel, California area. I should add that identifying fingerprints often takes quite a bit more time. In this case, we requested prints from the locksmith and the in-laws of Norma Widick who rode in the car to Las Vegas. The fingerprints of those individuals are not on file in the FBI data base. We needed to match any unknown fingerprints to a person. We were able to match all fingerprints lifted from the victim's car. We did not find any other prints including those of the victim's husband, Gaynard Widick. That came as no surprise as he probably does not use his wife's car."

Next, the prosecution called the first officer that reported to the crime scene on Blue Diamond Road. The officer, Joe Flinn, went into detail how he secured the crime scene and logged everyone in and out of the area that needed to examine the bodies, or any part of the taped off crime area.

The Medical Examiner followed and gave testimony to the condition of the bodies and how he determined the cause and time of death, including the trauma they suffered. He went into detail on the cause of the lacerations on the older victim's head and the bruises and rape of the younger victim.

Entering the third week of the trial, the defense continued to make objections in attempt to undermine the credibility of the prosecution's witnesses. The prosecution presented voluminous evidence tying the defendant to the murders.

The Assistant DA said to the judge, "I have two more expert witnesses that I will call to the stand. When they are through, the prosecution will rest."

Prior to the trial, Lingreen met with the expert witnesses that she planned to call to the witness stand. She told the two FBI agents that they would be called upon last. Both agents were meticulous in their evaluations of the crime and they had years of experience in the courtroom. After explaining to the agents how she wanted to wrap up the trial, agent Cochran said, "I applaud you for your diligence in handling this case. We want this guy put away as much as you do. There is no doubt that he would kill again if given the chance and we would probably be the ones that have to track him down."

Lingreen asked FBI Special Agent, Jay Cochran, to the stand. She introduced the agent as a ballistics and weapons expert. The prosecutor asked the agent when he began working for the FBI and to describe his primary duties at the agency.

"I began working for the FBI almost seventeen years ago. I spent four years in the Marine Corp. After my service as a Marine, I returned to college. I heard of an opportunity to apply for work at the bureau and I acted on that opportunity. I spent 20 weeks at Quantico and passed the induction test and physical and immediately after that I began working for the FBI. Practically all my training in ballistics and weaponry were taught to me at the bureau," said Cochran.

"Thank you, please describe the FBI findings regarding this murder scene and cause of death to the victims," said Lingreen.

The defense objected to the question, stating that the cause of death had already been agreed upon: both victims died by a gunshot to the head.

The prosecution argued that the testimony to be given by the agent describes the way in which the victims were shot, where the suspect positioned himself prior to the shootings, and what the suspect did to the bodies after he dumped them on the roadway. Lingreen told the judge, "Within days of the murders the LVPD requested assistance from the FBI. A serious and qualified concern arose that the LVPD may have a serial killer in custody. Additionally, there could be victims in multiple states. The FBI is the foremost agency in deploying rapid response and verification. Allow me to continue so the jurors can hear that the testimony from the Clark County Medical Examiner is reiterated and confirmed by the FBI."

The judge overruled the objection, and said he would allow the testimony.

The agent began by describing how the FBI determined that a specific bullet came from a specific firearm. He used visual aids to demonstrate etchings on bullets, and how they matched up perfectly to etchings on the inside of a gun barrel. The agent left no doubt in the minds of the jury that the gun confiscated by the police is the same gun used to commit the murders.

Agent Cochran described how the FBI, in cooperation with the local authorities, re-created what happened to the victims the moment the suspect fired the gun. The photos of the head shots of the victims would not be shown to the jury by previous agreement between the prosecution and the defense. But the FBI agent's verbal description left no doubt as to what happened to them when they were shot at point blank range.

Agent Cochran continued, "Mrs. Malloy, the older victim, met her fate by way of a gun shot in the back of the head. The assailant would have been in the back of the car, or the back seat of the car. We concluded that the assailant would be right-handed. We can determine that by the trajectory of the bullet, where it entered the skull and at what angle. Pieces of hair were extracted from the driver's side upper seat area. The hair would have come from the tight-fisted grip the accused applied to the victim's hair and scalp. Her head would have been pulled slightly backwards.

"The accused pressed the gun barrel against Mrs. Malloy's head at about ear level and just behind the right ear. That is a thick part of the skull. The angle of the gun, we determined was aimed upward at about a 6-to-8-degree angle. That would be consistent of someone holding the weapon in their right hand, sitting on a seat behind the victim, and pressing the gun barrel into the skull. We believe the victim, Mrs. Malloy, was unconscious or semi-conscious when the defendant shot her after an altercation moments earlier.

"The bullet discharged from the firearm and entered the head area as I described, but it did not exit the skull. Bone and mass slowed the bullet after impact. It lodged just beneath the left eye socket. It would have exited between the left eye and left ear. Due to the victim being older, the skull being thicker, and the gun fired as the barrel pressed against the skull, the bullet remained in the head cavity. The bullet extracted by the coroner matched accurately, 100% accurately, to the murder weapon found in possession of the accused." The agent stared directly at the defendant.

Then he shifted his gaze back to the jurors and said, "The bullet does not simply enter, or pass-through bone and flesh. It traumatizes the body. The projectile spreads out on impact and leaves a wide berth of destruction in its path. Mrs. Malloy bled from both ears, her left eye, and profusely from the entry wound. The heart will also continue to work, even though it is for only a short time after such trauma. It might beat for a few seconds before it stops. Blood is pumped into and out of the damaged area. The body does not bleed after it is dead. After being shot, Mrs. Malloy slumped to her right, toward her daughter. She bled for only a moment, enough to cause her blood to soak the front seat of the death car."

The Assistant DA waited a moment after the agent's testimony to allow the graphic description to resonate amongst the jury. The prosecutor also thought briefly that she was glad that the lead detective, Frieler, requested FBI oversight on this murder. The expert witness for the prosecution left little to no opportunity for the defense to object to the testimony. She knew that her witnesses were vetted by the defense, but they would seek every opportunity to discredit the police officers for not having the best equipment, or enough experience in their background to draw such conclusions. The agent, no stranger to the courtroom, provided no wiggle room for the defense to object when the agent began his testimony. The credentials, the training, the resources brought to bear by the FBI statements, and detailed description, all but eliminated objections of this witness. She silently thanked Detective Frieler for making this part of her job a little easier.

Assistant DA Lingreen asked the agent to describe the shooting death of the second victim; Norma Widick.

"Mrs. Widick, the younger victim, appears to have been in an escape mode and shot from 8 to 12 inches away from her head. The assailant would have been sitting more to the left side, or drivers' side, of the back seat behind the driver of the vehicle. The same location where he sat when he shot the first victim. The defendant raped the younger victim after neutralizing her mother. At that point he made a conscious decision to kill them both."

The defense objected saying that it is not possible for the agent to know that the killer made a conscious decision to execute the women.

The judge sustained the objection and said to strike the last comment from the record.

Lingreen asked the agent to continue.

Cochran said, "Mrs. Malloy, after being shot slumped to her right toward the passenger seat where her daughter sat."

The defense objected again stating that there is no way that the expert witness can claim that the younger victim saw her mother slump to the right after being shot.

The prosecution argued that the court already established that the first victim, Mrs. Malloy, did slump and fall to her right. That's how her blood stained the front seat of the vehicle.

Judge Novickas overruled the objection and told the agent to continue.

Agent Cochran resumed, "The younger victim saw her mother slump in the seat next to her. Traumatized and bruised from just being raped and man-handled, she then tried in vain to exit the vehicle. She clearly tried to escape the same fate as that of her mother. She managed to open the door, but did not get a foot outside the car. When the assailant saw her desperate attempt to run, he swung his right hand, still holding the gun, in her direction. She would have been leaning forward in her effort to exit the vehicle. She's younger and her skull would be softer than the older victim. Our skulls become thicker as we age. He fired the weapon at the back of her head. The bullet entered the left side of her skull, just below the left ear, a much softer part of the head cavity. Leaning forward to escape the car and the assailant, the bullet exited her skull on the right side, just below her right eye. That bullet shattered the window. The bullet also took parts of her flesh, blood and hair. Since she attempted to exit the vehicle, the force of the bullet added to that motion. Her head hit the inside of the door panel where tissue, and blood samples were found and collected, and were determined to have been that of the younger victim."

The agent's testimony of the two murders lasted nearly six hours that included the showing of visual aids, questions by the prosecutor and cross examination by the defense. The agent left no doubt about the brutality and gruesomeness of the crime scene. The prosecutor wanted the jury to feel what the victims must have felt like in the final moments of their lives. She wanted the jury to understand what a senseless, vicious, deliberate act the defendant launched, and now two very beautiful, innocent people were gone forever. She believed the physical evidence and testimonies she delivered would undisputedly tie the defendant to the crime.

The graphic and methodical description of the murders caused some jurors to squirm in their chairs. But Lingreen wasn't through, she would call upon one more qualified expert witness.

Just past 4:00 p.m., Judge Novickas adjourned the trial for the day.

"We will resume the trial tomorrow morning at 9:00 a.m.," he said.

CHAPTER FORTY

Last Moments

Gaynard Widick sat in the courtroom the previous day for Agent Cochran's testimony. The heinous murders, descriptions of the bodies, and horrific final moments of the victims' lives were causing him enormous grief. His young wife, kidnapped, beaten, raped and shot in the head is an unimaginable ending to such an energetic and caring person. He believed his actions set the killings in motion. He knew the grief his in-laws were experiencing, especially his father-in-law, Tom Malloy. Both of his parents sat in the courtroom with him and heard how brutal and terrifying those final moments were for Inez and Norma. Gaynard and his parents did not return to the courtroom the next day.

Judge Novickas brought the trial to order at exactly 9:00 a.m. He asked the Assistant DA if she would be bringing her final witness to the stand.

The DA affirmed that she would. She called FBI Agent, Paul Stombaugh, to the stand. Agent Stombaugh worked in the forensic division of the FBI regarding, fingerprints, blood and tissue analysis, and crime scene evaluation.

"Agent Stombaugh," Lingreen began, "please tell the court how long you have been employed by the FBI."

"It's been eighteen years. I went to work for the bureau just after World War II. I just completed college and received my teaching credential when the war broke out. I enlisted in the U.S. Army, and spent three years in combat in Europe. I also received my training in fingerprinting, blood and tissue analysis from the bureau."

"You have heard the testimony of the LVPD, the Clark County Sheriff's Department, the Medical Examiner, and that of FBI Agent Jay Cochran. Do you agree to the findings of those previous testimonies?" asked Lingreen.

"Absolutely," said the agent. "We, the FBI, were not the first on the scene. We were asked to come in after the fact to validate the findings of those that were previously discussed. We were also made aware of the LVPD's concerns regarding the younger victim's husband and of possible interstate killings. The LVPD and Clark County Sheriff's Office did quite a good job of collecting evidence, protecting the crime scene, and taking photographs of the evidence."

"Over the past three days of trial, the Clark County Sheriff's Department, the Medical Examiner, and FBI Special Agent Cochran, gave us a look into the final moments of the victims lives and explained how the victims were murdered. Agent Cochran systematically showed the jury how ballistics tie bullets and shell casings to a murder weapon. Can you tell us what role you played in examining the evidence?" asked Lingreen.

The agent took his time before responding. He noticed the reporters were eagerly waiting for his comments. The accused sat in his chair, both hands on the defense table, staring at the agent.

Then he glanced at the assistant DA before settling his gaze upon the jury. He said, "We examined and confirmed what the local forensic labs determined. The blood found in the vehicle belonged to the victims, as it matched their blood type. We also matched the hair found in the vehicle to be that of the two women. You heard testimony earlier that the younger victims' hair is a more auburn/brown color. We found fragments of her hair embedded in the front windshield and scattered among the glass fragments found in the car.

"We found a darker/reddish hair on the seat nearer the driver's location. That hair belonged to the older victim. Fragments of her hair were found on the back of the driver's seat and on the front seat where she slumped over. Fragments of her hair and blood were found on the asphalt road where her body had been dumped. We also found fragments of the victims' hair and blood on the shirt that belonged to the accused. The hair and the blood were most likely caused by the blow-back from the firing of the gun, the impact of the bullet hitting the skull at close range. The blowback of hair, blood and tissue got on the assailant's clothes. As identified earlier by the Medical Examiner, we confirmed the tissue samples removed from under the fingernails of the younger victim as belonging to the accused. The younger victim showed signs of trauma on her arms, legs and the left side of her face. That would be indicative of being hit with a fist or slapped hard with an open right hand. The face trauma is independent of the gunshot wound. The victim fought back when the accused grabbed her and began to rape her. She scratched his face and his left arm. Her left arm would have been pinned under her or pinned against the seat. She flailed at the assailant with her right-hand leaving scratch marks on the left side of the accused." Large photos of the defendant were placed on an easel for the jury to see the scratch marks on his face and arm. The photos were taken on the day of his arrest. "We also found fingerprints on both purses, and on their contents scattered about the crime scene. The fingerprints matched those of the defendant.

"We know that the older victim, Mrs. Malloy, was either unconscious or semi-conscious during the rape of her daughter. A struggle broke out between the older victim and the accused. He hit her repeatedly with the butt end of the gun on the right side of her head. This caused several lacerations and bleeding. He became enraged at both women. Once he knocked out the older victim, he dragged the younger victim out of the front seat of the car and forcefully threw her into the back of the car where he proceeded to rape her. She fought him the best she could, causing the scratch marks. Enraged even further by this, he yanked her out of the back seat, pushed and threw her into the front seat of the car. At this point the younger victim would be extremely traumatized by the beating, rape and witnessing of her mother being knocked unconscious and left bleeding in the drivers side of the front seat.

"The accused, angered by his struggle with the older victim and being scratched up by the younger victim crawled back into the rear of the car to retrieve his gun. He then grabbed the older victim by the hair on her head, pulled her head backwards and shot her. Within seconds, maybe less, the younger victim met the same fate: she attempted to flee the vehicle only to get a gunshot to the head." The agent shifted his gaze back to the accused and held it on him for a moment.

"Our evaluation of the crime scene led us to examine the particles of sand on the floor, in the carpet of the car on the driver's side. Particles of this sand were also found in the heels of the Oxford style shoes that belonged to the accused."

Defense attorney Wright objected on the grounds that sand is found everywhere in the desert around Las Vegas. The victims could have carried the sand into the car and the suspect could have picked up sand in his shoes from just about anywhere.

Lingreen asked the agent if all sand is the same.

The agent said, "We compared the sand where the women were found to the sand in the car and on the shoes of the defendant. You might think sand is sand, but in reality, there are many differences in size and composition. The sand that we examined all came from the same source: the crime scene site."

Upon cross-examination, Wright asked the agent to describe the crime scene when he arrived.

"We were not involved in the investigation until Tuesday, four days after the crime occurred. To answer your question, there was no crime scene when we entered the case, other than the specific location. The bodies and the evidence were removed soon after forensics completed their work. Once the FBI received a call to assist in the investigation, I did visit the crime location. Local law enforcement officials accompanied me and I reviewed the photos taken at the specific site, including photos of the death car which is also part of the crime scene."

"We heard earlier that when Detective Frieler arrived at the scene, he saw quite a few vehicles already on site; forensics, the M.E., the deputy sheriff and the police officers. Wouldn't it be impossible to keep a crime scene from being contaminated when that many people are parading through the site?" asked Wright.

"First responders are well versed on the need to keep a crime scene as clean as humanly possible. They must access the area and check on the victims. They are aware of where they step and what they touch. The teams that come in right behind the first responders are usually the ones that have given instructions to those that are first on the scene regarding what to do and what not to do. Fortunately, in this case, the Clark County Sheriff's Office and the LVPD are both very familiar about crime scene protocol. I can tell you from first-hand experience that they were cognizant not to allow contamination of the crime scene. If the crime occurred in a different place at a different time, it might be possible that 1,000 people could have contaminated the site. That did not happen. The murders were committed in an isolated area," said Cochran.

"Agent Cochran, we know that a private citizen came upon the crime scene first." Wright looked at his notes and said, "Bruce Cook made a phone call to the Clark County Sherriff's Office to report what he believed to be two bodies lying along the roadway. How could you possibly know that Bruce Cook did not contaminate the site, or if someone else could have been there that we don't even know about?"

"Mr. Cook's testimony revealed that he did not touch the bodies or any evidence around the crime scene. As I stated earlier, we examined and lifted fingerprints from the evidence. There were no unmatched prints on any of the evidence. Forensics found no footprints, or tire prints, that would add to the theory that someone else might have entered the crime scene before the police arrived," said Cochran.

"No more questions," said Wright.

Lingreen kept an eye on the jury during cross examination while seated in her chair. She felt that by the looks on their faces, the evidence and testimonies connecting the defendant to the murders were leaving no doubt of his guilt. Then she stood and asked the agent if he would tell the jury about the findings on the victims clothing.

"We examined the clothing that both women were wearing, first as part of the blood and tissue analysis. The LVPD, and Clark County Forensic teams said they discovered what appeared to be tire tracks on the women's clothing. They were correct. The markings on their clothing matched the tire tread on the 1957 Chevy. The accused shot both women while they were seated inside the vehicle.

"Then the suspect pulled both victims from the car and left them on the edge of the road. The two bodies were approximately 15 feet apart. That's due to them being pulled from each side of the vehicle. The younger victim's body laid partially on the asphalt road and partially on desert sand.

"The accused attempted to turn the vehicle in a left angle to the travel lanes. He did this so he could maneuver the car on the asphalt and turn it around without driving onto the sandy area and risk getting stuck. In his effort to do that, the left rear tire of the vehicle ran over the older victim, causing post-mortem injuries. He backed the vehicle up to turn it around and keep it on the asphalt. When he backed it up, the right rear tire hit the younger victim leaving an imprint on her clothing. This time, the car did not completely run over the body. The driver then made a sharp left turn and headed back toward Las Vegas.

"On the far side of the road, the opposite side, the forensic team took photos of tire tracks that were off the pavement and ran into the sand. The tire tracks proved to match those of the right front tire of the car."

Questions and cross examination of the witness lasted until early afternoon. The prosecution told the court they were finished and would bring no more testimony before the court. They rested their case at 2:45 p.m.

Judge Novickas looked at both attorneys for the defense and said, "The psychological evaluation team for the defense has informed my office they need at least three, maybe four, more weeks to complete their analysis on the mental state of the defendant. That will move the findings on the defendant's mental health status to mid-June as the earliest possible schedule date. In the event the defendant is found guilty on any or all charges brought against him by the DA's office, the penalty or sentencing phase of this trial will not occur until after we have heard from the mental health experts. Do either of you have any questions or comments about that process?"

Defense Attorney Wright stood and said, "My client should be remanded to a state mental hospital for mental evaluation and recovery. He is not fit to stand trial."

"So noted. That decision will not be made until the court has heard evaluations from both sides on the subject of your client's mental health. Until then, he will remain in custody of the Clark County Sheriff," said the judge.

"Now, moving along, the prosecution has rested. Does the defense wish to have any further witnesses give testimony?"

The defense submitted three names during the discovery process to the court and to the DA's office of whom they might call to the witness stand. The first being a law professor at the Nevada State University. Attorney Wright hoped to draw attention to the search and seizure of the death vehicle without a warrant. He wanted to plant the seed of malfeasance on the LVPD in the minds of the jury. However, he made the claim of an illegal search and seizure early in the trial. The judge ruled there were no violations incurred by the LVPD. They were well within their legal rights to search and seize the car based on improper identification of car ownership. Bringing someone in to further exacerbate that issue would more than likely work against the defense. Cross examination by the Assistant DA could make the law professor look like a witness for the prosecution.

The second name on the witness list showed him to be a lab technician who worked for a nearby pharmaceutical company. The defense planned to break down the testimony of the prosecutions forensic team's findings by identifying all the things that can taint proper lab work. Thus, discrediting the findings of the local and federal investigators.

The lab tech informed Defense Attorneys Wright and McGinnis that his testimony might backfire. Cross examination by the prosecutor would ferret out anything the defense witness would do differently than what the LVPD and FBI presented. The LVPD and the county knew the importance of a sterile environment for accurate lab work. The FBI knew it better than anyone.

Wright also thought about the awkward situation he found himself in regarding the forensic books that belong to Deputy Mallinger. During the time set aside for the defense to prepare their witnesses, the lab tech convinced the defense attorney that his testimony would probably not help. He did not get called to the stand.

The third person that the defense proposed to call was the parking lot attendant who reported the car as being suspicious. The defense told the court they reserved the right to cross examine this individual, whose name appeared on the list for the prosecution.

Recalling the parking lot attendant to the stand, Wright said, "Mr. Long, your statement to the police said that you witnessed the 1957 Chevy, the car in question, enter the parking lot around 1:30 a.m., on the night of the murders. Is that correct?"

"Yes, it is," said Long.

"How many people did you see in the vehicle that night? One? Two? Three? How many people were in that vehicle when it pulled into the parking lot?"

"I don't know. I only saw the driver," said Long.

"You only saw the driver, but you could not identify him. Is that correct?"

"Yes, like I said before, I did not get a good look at him. It was late and dark."

"So, there could have been more than one passenger in that vehicle?"

The prosecution objected, asking the court to tell the People of Nevada where the defense could possibly be going with this line of questioning.

"Your Honor," said Wright, "I am wanting to establish that the only person who saw the vehicle in question, cannot tell the court how many people were in that car. My client could not be positively identified as the driver of the vehicle the night of the alleged crime. The police arrested him for trying to take the vehicle, which he said he borrowed, out of the parking lot. We don't know who parked that car at that hour."

Lingreen shouted, "Objection! That's ridiculous. The court has heard from expert forensic fingerprint analysts. He stated there were *no unidentified fingerprints* in the vehicle. This is quite a leap by the defense to be suggesting that his client did not park the car and maybe, let me stress the *maybe part*, there was more than one passenger, suggesting an accomplice or more than one accomplice? That somehow, someone else possessed the keys to the car and perpetrated the crime? Is that what we are expected to believe? Are we going to start chasing mythical or imaginary scenarios?"

Judge Novickas spoke next. "Mr. Wright and Mr. McGinnis, do you have any evidence, any proof at all that links this crime to more than one person, or that there is proof of more than one person in the vehicle when it entered the parking lot on the night of the murders?"

Wright responded, "Your Honor, the court just heard the parking lot attendant say he could not identify my client. Everything presented by the prosecution has been purely circumstantial. I want the jury to know there is reasonable doubt about the prosecution pinning the crime solely on my client.

The Assistant DA did not bring proof of a motive, nor did she provide any eye witnesses to the crime. And, the one person who they claim initiated the arrest of my client, the parking lot attendant, could not identify him either."

"Objection sustained. Do you have any more questions of this witness?" asked Judge Novickas.

"No," said Wright.

Do you have any more witnesses you wish to examine?"

"The defense rests, Your Honor. However, we want to go on record as opposing the procedure for this trial," said Wright.

"Noted," said the judge. He then slowly turned in his chair to face the jury panel. He told them the prosecution and the defense would make closing arguments to the jury. After that, the jury would be sequestered, so they could enter deliberations in order to render a decision on the guilt or innocence of the defendant.

The prosecutor stood to present her closing arguments.

Lingreen spoke to the jury for nearly 30 minutes. She reminded them that by agreement between the defense and the prosecution, photos of the victims' heads would not be shown. Two large photos of Inez Malloy and Norma Widick were placed on easels, so the jury could see the victims before they were shot. Norma's photo, her high school graduation picture, showed a young, beautiful, smiling woman. Inez's photo, a portrait of her and Tom, taken almost 2 years earlier.

Lingreen identified each of the victims. "Inez Malloy; wife, mother, sister, daughter, aunt, grandmother, godmother, and friend of many. Norma Widick; wife, daughter, cousin, aunt, co-worker, her whole life still ahead of her. These two beautiful women were unrecognizable after the brutal car-jacking and deadly assault by the defendant."

She explained how the defendant got into the victim's car, how he planned to take them out of town and execute them for a few dollars. He tried to claim the vehicle belonged to his girlfriend—another of his many false stories.

Methodically, Lingreen put the time line together, day by day, hour by hour, minute by minute.

Then she re-capped the indisputable evidence and the painstaking work by the forensic team and the FBI. While making her case before the jury, she frequently referenced the photos of the victims, reminding the jury of the loss to loved ones.

"Members of the jury," said Lingreen, "Roy Warren Osborn committed a senseless, selfish and horrific murderous crime. The LVPD caught him in possession of the victim's vehicle, which is *grand theft*. He bludgeoned Inez Malloy knocking her unconscious, raped her daughter, Norma Widick. Then he murdered them, rifled through their purses, took their money and tossed the purses into the desert. Then as he left in Norma Widick's car, he ran over the victims and left them lying dead in the desert amid the contents of their purses.

"He drove away, hoping to get away clean. He did not get very far. The defense wanted a motive. You have it, you've had it all along: It's *robbery*. That is the motive behind his actions that fateful night. He picked two innocent women to rob at gun point, but that would not be enough for him. As you heard the expert witness: he pistol whipped one of them knocking her unconscious, raped the other, shot them both in the head and then ran over them using the stolen get-a-way car. The defendant has no regard for the life of others and he put that on full display just over a year ago in the Nevada desert. For what? A little bit of money and a get-away car?

"The defense asked you to believe there were no eye-witnesses to the murders." She walked slowly over to the defense table. "There is one." She turned her gaze directly at the defendant and the jury followed her gaze. "Only this eye-witness does not want to talk to you. We do not need him to take the stand since he has chosen not to. The evidence and the expert testimonies presented to you prove, without any doubt, that this man; Roy Warren Osborn killed those two women in cold blood and without remorse. The evidence presented to you and the re-creation of the crime scene, the terror the two women experienced at the hands of this killer, speak volumes and they speak for the two women."

She paused for a moment to allow the jury to soak that in. Then she gestured toward the defense table, "The defendant is a callous and cold-blooded killer. I am sure that throughout this trial you have noticed he has shown no remorse for the crimes he committed.

"In my opening comments to you, I said we would provide to you the evidence, overwhelming evidence, allowing you to choose two first-degree murder convictions. We have delivered that information to you." She paused, then said, "Thank you for being here, and thank you for your service to the community." Lingreen turned slowly and walked back to her chair.

The defense attorney then stood before the jury. Attorney Wright told them that they just heard a dramatic plea by the prosecution that pointed to his client as being the guilty party in the double killings. He stressed the issues that he brought up repeatedly during the trial; the prosecution could not produce an eye witness and the prosecution could only grab at a potential motive for the crimes. He also reminded the jury that his client has repeatedly claimed his innocence from the moment he was arrested for alleged car theft. Standing before the jury, Wright reminded them that his client continued to maintain his innocence.

"I know I do not need to remind you of the heavy burden and responsibility placed upon each of you. That burden would weigh exponentially heavier if you were to render a wrongful conviction, potentially sending the accused to death row for something he did not do. I implore you, ladies and gentlemen of the jury, to discard the unproven and circumstantial debate you heard from the prosecution," said Wright.

Then he turned his attention to Judge Novickas and said, "The defense rests."

The judge nodded his head toward defense attorney Wright, acknowledging that the defense completed their closing statements. He then turned his gaze toward Lingreen and said, "You are allowed the final word, do you have anything further to say to the jury?"

Lingreen stood and then slowly walked over to the two photos of the murder victims. She positioned herself so the photos were just over her right shoulder and as she spoke to the jury, they would see the victims during the DA's closing statement.

"Ladies and Gentlemen of the jury, this young woman," she pointed to Norma Widick's photo, "twenty-two years old, her whole life ahead of her. Someday she planned on becoming an attorney and standing before a jury like you. Inez Malloy, fifty-three years old, enjoying a new chapter in her life involving three loving grand-children. These two women were violently ripped away from people that loved them, needed them, and counted on them.

"We have provided to you, the jury, absolute proof through the blood and fingerprint evidence, as well as ballistics confirmed by the FBI. The defendant did not admit to the crime even after being caught trying to reclaim the stolen car containing the evidence of the murders that he committed. This man must be taken off the streets and prevented from ever killing again," said Lingreen.

"Our nation has a pretty good judicial system, it is not perfect, but it is a good one. Based on biblical principles: thou shall not steal, thou shall not commit murder." She walked over and stood a few feet in front of the table where the defendant and his attorneys were sitting. She gestured with her hand in the direction of the defendant. "This man, Roy Warren Osborn, sitting before you today, deliberately chose to ignore the laws of the land. Not only did he fail to adhere to the laws that govern society, he failed miserably to recognize the laws of nature. From humans to the animal kingdom, from birds to mammals, a mother's instinct to protect their children, their offspring, is an incredible force of nature. You heard Agent Cochran testify earlier regarding the powerful instinct of a mom. Inez Malloy recognized this man for what he is; a thief, a liar, a rapist and a killer. She could not allow harm to come to her daughter without putting up a fight. She paid with her life protecting a life that is more precious than her own."

Then Lingreen moved her right arm and hand toward the two photos of the women and peered into the eyes of each of the 12 jurors. "Some of you probably have children and a spouse. It would not be difficult to relate to the devastating and long-lasting effect if they were senselessly murdered and taken from you. Ladies and Gentlemen, deliver justice for these two innocent and beautiful women and for their family. Put this man away forever, do not allow him to kill again."

Lingreen allowed a few moments to pass then she slowly walked back to the prosecution table and said to the judge, "The prosecution rests Your Honor."

The judge gave final instructions to the jury and told them their lunch would be brought to them. Their work would begin now regarding delibera-tions of the trial. He reminded them that any information they might need for further review would be brought to them by the bailiff, who would be stationed just outside their door.

Assistant DA Lingreen, and her legal assistant, Jolie Eimers, returned to their office. Now the wait would begin to find out how the jury would render a decision on this murder trial. She picked up the phone on her desk and dialed Tom Malloy's number.

Tom answered the phone and Lingreen said, "Tom, the trial is over and the jury has been sequestered. I do not know how long it will take them to bring a verdict back to the courtroom. I know this has been a long and difficult journey for you and your loved ones. I will let you know the moment we hear something from the courts."

"Yes, it has been a long time. It seems like a lifetime and it seems like only yesterday. Thank you for all you have done. I would like to be there for the verdict. I probably cannot make the drive but I will talk to my daughter and in-laws to let them know what you told me. I am sure some of them will want to be there and I will make every effort to be there also. I know you said you do not know when they will finish their discussion. Do you think it will be a week or longer? The drive over there is 4 ½ to 5 hours so if anyone wants to plan on going, they would have to be there before the jury brings a recommendation to the judge," said Tom.

"I doubt if it will take a week to make a decision. Three or four days might be long enough. You might tell your relatives that they should make plans to come to Las Vegas as soon as possible."

"Thanks, I will let everyone know," and they said goodbye. Tom let Margie know of the pending sentencing and asked her to pass on that information.

PART FIVE

CHAPTER FORTY-ONE

Jury Decision

After nearly 20 hours, just short of three days of deliberation, the jury foreman notified the bailiff that the jury reached a unanimous decision. The prosecutor and the defense counsel were notified and returned to the courthouse to hear the verdict. The jury filed into the courtroom, and the foreman handed the bailiff their decision. The bailiff handed the jury documents to the judge, who read them slowly, and carefully to himself.

Judge Novickas removed his reading glasses, turned in his chair toward the jury foreman, "Is this the unanimous decision of the jury?"

"Yes, Judge," replied the foreman.

Judge Novickas said, "Would the defendant please stand." Osborn stood up. The two attorneys representing him slowly rose out of their chairs and stood next to him, one on each side. The prosecution remained seated.

The judge then reminded everyone in the courtroom that there will not be any outbursts allowed when the verdict is read. Any such outbursts, and the individual will be immediately removed from the courtroom. He scanned the courtroom, looking from one side to the other. The victim's family and friends occupied most of the seats behind the prosecution. Members of the media often stood in the back of the courtroom, so they could exit quickly to call in updates on the trial or meet a deadline without causing too much of a disturbance.

There were no family members or friends of the defendant in the courtroom.

Judge Novickas scanned the jury papers again before he began to read the verdict to the crowded but silent courtroom.

"On the charge of first-degree murder in the slaying of Mrs. Inez Malloy, the jury finds the defendant . . . guilty as charged." The judge paused for a brief moment, he then asked each of the jurors individually if they agreed with the verdict. Each one responded that they did.

"On the second charge of first-degree murder in the slaying of Mrs. Norma Widick, the jury finds the defendant . . . guilty as charged." The judge asked each juror if they agree. Again, they said *yes*.

Judge Novickas leaned forward in his chair, resting his elbows on his bench. He adjusted his reading glasses and said, "On the charge of kidnapping Mrs. Inez Malloy, the jury finds the defendant . . . guilty as charged." The judge asked each juror individually if they agreed. They all confirmed that they did.

"On the charge of kidnapping Mrs. Norma Widick, the jury finds the defendant . . . guilty as charged." The judge again asked each juror to confirm that they were in agreement. They were all in agreement.

"On the charge of grand theft auto, the jury finds the defendant. . . guilty as charged." Judge Novickas polled each juror and they all confirmed the guilty verdict.

"On the charge of armed robbery of Mrs. Inez Malloy and Mrs. Norma Widick, the jury finds the defendant . . . guilty as charged." Again, the judge polled the jurors and they were all in agreement.

"On the final charge in the rape of Mrs. Norma Widick, the jury finds the defendant . . . guilty as charged." One by one the jurors confirmed they were in agreement.

The judge removed his reading glasses and turned to address the jury. Before he could, the courtroom exploded with movement and sound. Reporters were scurrying out the door to finalize their story about the jury's decision on this horrific double homicide. Other people in the courtroom stood up out of the chairs, talking to one another. Margie squeezed her father's arm and reached over the railing that separated the attendees from the attorneys. She hugged the assistant DA and said, "Thank you." Lingreen hugged Margie back, both women were emotionally drained and relieved. Tears welled in Margie's eyes, the DA hugged her tighter and whispered, "It's over, it's over."

Margie pulled back from the DA and said, "Only the trial is over."

Lingreen glanced over at Tom Malloy. He showed no emotion other than a slight nodding of his head. *Does that indicate he approves of the outcome of the trial? I don't know, he is a difficult man to read. I hope he can find his way through his grief.* She understood that the law would punish the killer for his crimes. But the grief that the family members would bear could not be eased through courtroom justice. Their losses were permanent.

The judge banged the gavel on his desk several times, loudly.

The room fell silent once again. He said, "Thank you, now please be seated. This trial has not yet been concluded." Then he turned his attention toward the defendant and said, "Roy Warren Osborn, a jury of your peers has found you *guilty on all seven charges.* Each of those charges are felonies in the State of Nevada. I hope you realize the gravity of the jury's decision to hold you accountable on each of these charges. Two of those charges allow the state to impose a sentence of death upon you. You will remain in custody of the Clark County Sheriff until I render the penalty phase of the verdict. I expect to have you back in my courtroom in less than one month's time, when we will hear from and review the findings of your mental evaluation. The defense has assured me that the evaluators will have completed their work by that time. The prosecution will also have completed their evaluation. In the meantime, you will be able to sit in the solitude of your jail cell and reflect on what transpired here today, and what you did that fateful night 15 months ago. I hope you find some peace now that the trial is over. God knows the victims had no peace that horrendous night and their families are still struggling to find peace and make sense of all this. Deputies, you will now take custody of the accused and escort him from the courtroom."

Judge Novickas turned in his chair and thanked the jury for their services recognizing how difficult this has been for each of them. Then he said, "You are now free to talk about the case if you choose to do so. I am going to have the bailiff escort you into the jury room. I will join you there in a few moments and answer any questions that you may have and thank you personally for your service. The jury stood up from their chairs and walked out of the courtroom into the jury chambers.

Before adjourning the trial, the judge reiterated that the mental evaluations by the defense and prosecutor will be ready for discussion in four weeks and will take place in this courtroom. He banged his gavel on the top of the bench concluding the murder trial.

Next, the decision on whether or not the defendant's mental wellness would allow the State of Nevada to invoke the death penalty.

CHAPTER FORTY-TWO

State of Mind

The defense attorneys and the prosecutor's office reached out to different institutions regarding an evaluation of the defendant. The defense sought input from the University of Nevada, Psychologist Dr. Henry Canon. The prosecution hired Dr. Ron Turner from Sacramento, California to examine the defendant.

Judge Novickas called the court to order on June 14th at exactly 9:00 a.m. Nearly fifteen months after the murders. He informed the defense attorneys and the prosecutors that the court will take testimony from their respective examiners. "Both sides will be allowed to cross examine. I have blocked out two days for testimony. I do not expect it to go any longer than that. Let us begin, Mr. Wright would you please call your witness first."

Defense Attorney Wright asked Dr. Henry Canon to the witness stand.

"Dr. Canon, please tell us your qualifications to evaluate the mental state of the defendant."

"I began my career with the State of Nevada right after graduating from the University of Nevada, Las Vegas 25 years ago. I worked at the State of Nevada Mental Hospital in Carson City. Shortly after that, I sought my Master Degree in Psychology then went on to complete my PhD in the same field. I have been a professor at the University of Nevada for the past 15 years. I frequently review cases to determine the level of an individual's ability to function on their own and make correct decisions."

"When did you first interview the defendant?" asked Wright.

"I spoke to the defendant for the first time less than 3 months ago. Since then I have met with him a total of seven times," said Dr. Canon.

"Can you describe for the court your opinion of the defendant's mental state throughout the time you spent evaluating him."

"The defendant has slowly but steadily regressed over the period of his incarceration. He does not have a firm grip on what is happening. At times, he seems to barely be in contact with reality. His recognition of reality seems to have loosened in the past several months. I could determine that he has a very high intelligence. However, he operates on very few cylinders. He crossed the borderline into becoming psychotic.

"As an individual, the defendant has a feeling of failure. He has few friends and a feeling that people are against him. Under the right circumstances, the defendant would be more dangerous than other people. The defendant has gone crazy. If he killed Inez Malloy and Norma Widick, he probably did not know right from wrong."

Dr. Canon's evaluation of the defendant lasted about 45 minutes. When he finished, Defense Attorney Wright thanked him for his time and then turned toward the judge. He said, "I would also like to submit a report from Dr. Marcus Pender of the Deter Clinic here in Las Vegas. This report reiterates the testimony we just heard from Dr. Canon." He handed the report to the court clerk and returned to his chair.

Lingreen stood and said, "Judge, I cannot cross examine a hand written report. This is a very important trial, and the defense attorney's client is facing the death penalty. Why isn't this individual in the courtroom so he can be questioned?"

Judge Novickas said, "There are probably many reasons, good reasons, the psychiatrist could not attend today's hearing. I will allow the written report. Do you have any questions for Dr. Canon?"

Assistant DA Lingreen paused for a brief moment. She picked up a file folder from her table then approached the witness stand. Thanking Dr. Canon for being here today she asked him if he needed anything, perhaps a glass of water. He declined, stating that he's fine.

Before Lingreen began her questioning she gave some background of the case.

"Dr. Canon, on March 27, fifteen months ago around midnight, the defendant committed an unspeakable crime of kidnapping at gunpoint, grand theft auto, robbery, rape, and the murder of two innocent women. You told the court that you began your examination of the defendant's mental state less than three months ago. Can you give us some insight into the defendant's state of mind at the time he committed the murders?"

A brief pause fell over the courtroom before Dr. Canon spoke. Then he said, "There is no way to know the state of mind of the defendant at the time the crimes were committed. There is no evaluation of his mental state at that time. An initial meeting took place ten weeks ago and a more thorough examination has been ongoing since that time. I have no doubt that being isolated from society, locked in a cell, no human contact, every day being the same, will alter a persons' state of mind in a negative way," said Dr. Canon.

"Dr. Canon," said Lingreen, "I want to draw your attention to a word you used in describing the defendants state of mind. As you are aware, the court is obligated to address the defendant's state of mind, his sanity, regarding this heinous crime. During your testimony, you said the defendant is 'crazy,' you did not use the word 'insane.' Crazy is a more generic term that can be applied to just about any circumstance, and any person, depending on what they might have just done, or said. Using the word, 'insane' is a very clear definition, it should be clear to the evaluators to carefully pick their words in a case that has such a high profile and consequences. You stated earlier that there is no way to know the state of mind of the defendant at the time of the murders. What would you say about his ability to distinguish right from wrong at the time of the murders?"

Dr. Canon said, "It would be difficult to determine if the defendant knew right from wrong at the time of the murders. His incarceration has taken a toll on his ability to think clearly. In my opinion, if the defendant did kill Mrs. Malloy and Mrs. Widick, he did not know right from wrong at the time of the murders. He could not have been in full control of his mental state due to the consumption of alcohol. The LVPD reported him to be inebriated at the time of his arrest. No one could have committed such a crime if they were thinking clearly."

Lingreen turned a paper over in her folder.

"Doctor, the defense would like to have the court declare the defendant legally insane. You have several methods of evaluating an individual's mental state. I am not a psychiatrist and make no claims to having any expertise in that field. But my understanding of the law is that in order to recommend, or declare, someone legally insane a person would have to have a background, or a history, of not knowing what they were doing when committing a crime. The defendant hid in the back of a car, possessed a gun and forced two women to drive out of town at gun point, beat one, raped the other, shot them both in the head and ran over them as he tried to speed away in the getaway car. That sounds to me like he put this plan in motion the moment he hid in the back of that car in the locksmith parking lot. Allow me to read a statement you made in your summary report to the court regarding the mental state of the defendant. *Quote: Osborn has a loose grip on reality, he is highly intelligent, but given the right circumstances he could be more dangerous than other people, end quote.* More dangerous than other people and highly intelligent . . . doesn't this mean that he has the capacity to know right from wrong? He certainly fits the description of being more dangerous than other people: double homicide, auto theft, kidnapping, rape and robbery. It is also important to point out that the accused has an extensive history of crime that spans over the past 25 years. Each of his crimes escalated in violence. He became more brazen, more arrogant, and showed no regard for human life."

Your Honor," said Defense Attorney Wright, "I would like to have the last comments from the prosecutor stricken from the record. Mr. Osborn is not on trial for any past crimes."

Judge Novickas peered at the defense attorney. "Mr. Wright, I appreciate the fact that you are listening intently to everything the prosecutor is saying. Let me remind you that this is not a trial, that ended four weeks ago. Today we are trying to determine the mental state of your client and whether or not the death penalty should be invoked as a result of the crimes. Your client's past behavior is important in helping the court, more specifically in helping me, to determine his sanity."

Turning in his chair he said to the prosecutor, "Please continue."

Lingreen said she did not have any more questions for the witness at this time.

Defense attorney Wright stood up and said, 'If it pleases the court, I have one more question of the witness."

The judge motioned for Wright to come forward.

"Dr. Canon, the prosecutor questioned your choice of words during the cross examination. Can you tell us why you described the defendant as crazy?"

"Crazy and insane can be interchangeable words. Both have the same meaning when describing a patient's mental state. Absurd, foolish, mad, erratic, nuts can be words to describe a state of mind. I chose 'crazy' due to how I perceived the defendant becoming as a result of his lengthy incarceration."

"Thank you," said Wright.

The judge dismissed the witness and asked the prosecution to bring in their examiner.

Lingreen introduced Dr. Ron Turner. He stood at the witness stand and the bailiff swore him in like all the witnesses before him.

"Dr. Turner," said Lingreen. "You heard the testimony from the defense witness regarding the mental state of the accused. Would you tell us your opinion of the defendant's state of mind at the time of the killings?"

"It is impossible to gauge the defendant's sanity at the time of the slayings. There is no evaluation of the defendant at that time. I did contact the Oregon State Penal system and spoke to their psychologist. Osborn received counseling while incarcerated in Oregon. The summation of their analysis is that he displayed a high level of animosity toward authority. He is a loner and saw a total of three visitors during the five-year period of imprisonment in Oregon. The evaluations we did came well after a year of him being incarcerated here in Nevada. Being separated from social interaction, and not being able to move about freely, will have an impact on an individual's state of mind. However, his state of mind at the time of the killings is completely unknown," said Turner.

"Thank you," said Lingreen.

Then pivoting, she addressed the judge and said, "The defendant is on trial for what he did on March 27th, fifteen months ago. The evaluators for the defense have suggested that the state of mind of the defendant is largely due to his being incarcerated. He was not incarcerated when he killed these two women. Both profiles, one from the defense, and one from the prosecution, concur that there is no way to know his state of mind fifteen months ago. The defense suggested that the accused must have been intoxicated at the time of the murders and did not know right from wrong. We do not know his level of intoxication at the time of the murders. We know of his intoxication at the time of his arrest, but several hours passed between the murders and the arrest, giving him plenty of time to consume alcohol."

Defense Attorney Wright stood and said, "Your Honor, it is clear that the mental capacity of my client is diminished, and he cannot be held accountable for a double homicide. I motion that capital punishment not be allowed as penalty for the crime, and that my client be remanded to a state mental hospital."

Judge Novickas said, "I am going to deny your motion at this time. Please continue with the cross examination."

Wright continued to argue his plea to the judge, "My client is obviously unable to make correct decisions. I implore you, Your Honor, to send him to a state mental institution until such time that he can reasonably re-enter society."

"Please be seated Mr. Wright, so we can continue," said the judge.

The discussion, testimony and cross examination on the defendant's mental capacity lasted until early afternoon. The only common ground between the opposing views is that it would be impossible to gauge the defendant's sanity at the time of the killings.

By 3:00 p.m. the defense attorney and the prosecution exhausted their arguments on the defendant's sanity.

Judge Novickas said, "I will adjourn this session for the rest of the afternoon. I want to thank everyone for being here and providing testimony today. We will reconvene tomorrow morning at 9:00 a.m. at which time I will render my opinion on the insanity plea."

The judge tapped his gavel on the bench, and like the jury trial ended, the reporters moved very quickly to leave the building and report on the sanity arguments.

CHAPTER FORTY-THREE

Sentencing

T he following morning, Judge Novickas tapped his gavel on the bench and the insanity hearing began at 9:00 a.m.

The judge gazed across the courtroom then shifted his attention to the defendant for a few moments before he spoke. The courtroom seated noticeably fewer attendees than during the jury trial.

Then the judge said, "I have conferred with my colleagues who were also involved in this case and have spoken to Mr. Osborn. Their interaction came shortly after his arrest. They described the accused as being 'in control' of his thoughts and actions." The judge glanced around the room before he continued.

"Shortly after your arrest, and before the preliminary hearing, you requested that you be allowed to represent yourself in this trial. You have the right to do that. However, during the interaction between yourself and District Judge Zenoff, you were advised that it would not be in your best interest to represent yourself. Judge Zenoff further explained that the Justice of the Peace assigned you a defense attorney to advise you during the preliminary trial so your constitutional rights were not violated.

"I also reviewed the correspondence between yourself and the district judge, when you requested a separate attorney to represent you during the preliminary hearings for each of the murders. That seems to be an acknowledgement, on your part, to accept court appointed defense. The court does not know, and will not know your state of mind at the time of the murders. However, the State of Nevada will not allow capital punishment of any person that may have a diminished mental capacity. I am going to reiterate that the court does not know your state of mind fifteen months ago. We heard from an expert witness for the defense yesterday concurring that it is not possible to determine your state of mind at the time of the murders. We heard from the testimony that an obvious change appeared in your mental state during the evaluation. Quoting Dr. Canon: 'you are highly intelligent but not operating on all cylinders.' Stating again that this is likely due to your incarceration and isolation from society. Therefore, I am removing the death penalty from the sentencing.

"However, you will not be sent to a state mental hospital either. I am sentencing you to two consecutive life sentences: one for each of the murders that you committed. You will be remanded to the Nevada State Penitentiary for the remainder of your life without the possibility of parole for auto theft, kidnapping, robbery and the murders of Mrs. Inez Malloy and the rape of Mrs. Norma Widick."

The defense attorneys and the prosecutor remained silent. The defendant stared at the judge.

Judge Novickas said, "Mr. Osborn, do you have anything to say to the court before you are removed and taken back to your cell?"

In a display of arrogance, and one that did not allude to possible insanity, the defendant said, "I am not guilty of any of these charges. I want the defense attorneys terminated from my case, and I want new attorneys appointed, so I can appeal the unfairness of this sentence."

The reporters once again scurried out of the courtroom.

Judge Novickas said, "Mr. Osborn, that is your prerogative to appeal your sentencing. I wish you all the best pursuing that endeavor. Bailiff, please remove the defendant. Court adjourned." He hit his gavel on the bench just one time then he stood and walked out of the courtroom.

Eventually, a new defense attorney was assigned to the accused. The new attorney wrote a summary appeal to the Nevada Supreme Court. He argued that the gun, and other evidence used against his client were obtained from an illegal search.

The defense also argued that the jury misstated information when they got the names of the two women reversed. The jury said they found the defendant guilty of first-degree murder in the slaying of Inez Widick, and the slaying of Norma Malloy. The victims last names somehow got reversed in the transcripts: Inez Malloy and Norma Widick were the correct names, even though Norma's birth name is Norma Malloy. The defense attorney said that the clerical error prevented his client from being charged for the two murders. He went on to say in his summary paper that the verdict would have to be set aside.

Two months after the verdict and the penalty of two consecutive life sentences without the possibility of parole, the Supreme Court of Nevada upheld the verdict. The justices on the Supreme Court of Nevada ruled the search to be legal because the car did not belong to the defendant. The judges also said that the reversal of the names is a clerical error, and would not change the outcome of the verdict.

The convicted murderer would appeal his sentence a total of seven times during his incarceration. Every appeal would be ruled frivolous and denied. In 1984, twenty years after the murders, he appealed to have time spent in custody: predisposition confinement. The attorneys working for the public defender's office requested to the Nevada Supreme Court that the 456 days the accused spent in confinement be credited to his sentence. The argument from the defense stated that the defendant did not have the opportunity to post bail, even though the JP denied bail at the initial appearance. The additional confinement to be held until the trial occurred caused an additional suffering upon the defendant for the crime. The defense went on to say that the results of the sentence would be intolerable and repugnant to both the Nevada Constitution and the United States Constitution, running afoul of both the Double Jeopardy and Due Process provisions of both documents.

The District Attorney's office responded to the appeal by saying it is an absurd request. The defendant received two life sentences without the possibility of parole. Excusing the 456 days of custody prior to his sentencing would not make any difference in the length of his sentence. Since (at least in theory) he will never be released, there is neither need for, nor purpose in, granting credit for time served. He added that the accused will not serve a shorter sentence and thereby will not be eligible for anything any earlier. The prosecutor stated the appeal to be frivolous, and it should be denied.

The Nevada Supreme Court ruled on the appeal by stating that the court recognizes the fact that incarceration of any kind is generally punitive in nature. As legal commentators have noted, the denial of credit for dead time—time spent in incarceration before delivery of the defendant to the State Prison—is basically a failure to recognize the punitive aspect of pre-disposition confinement. The court granted the credit for time served prior to the sentencing, 456 days.

Shortly after the murders, Mitchell Malloy was arrested for possession of a controlled substance: cocaine. The charges included possession and distribution. He could not make bail, set at $25,000. He called his Uncle Chuck and asked if he could help. The bail amount required collateral.

Chuck asked his wife, "Would you mind if we took out a second mortgage on the house to get Mitchell out of jail until his trial date?"

Without hesitation she said, "No, I don't want any part of that. I'm afraid he would skip bail, and we would be stuck making good on the payment." Chuck did not share the same concern, but he did not press the issue.

He went to the L.A. County Detention Center to meet with Mitchell. He told him, "I am not going to be able to raise the bail money without mortgaging the house. That would create a bit of domestic unrest, and I don't want to go there. You told me not to notify your old man of your predicament, but that may be the only option. He could possibly take a second mortgage on his house."

Mitchell shook his head. "I'm probably going to have to sit here until my trial date in a few weeks. My dad does not need the disappointment of my arrest heaped onto the weight of the murders."

"Suit yourself, if there is anything you need, give me a holler," said Chuck.

The judge sentenced Mitchell to two years of incarceration minus time served: 47 days.

His release came less than a year later. The penal system allows credit for time served combined with good behavior and participation in recommended programs. Most prisoners will only serve half the amount of their sentence unless it is for a violent crime.

After his release, Mitchell did not contact any of his relatives for the next 13 years. Tom Malloy made every attempt to re-engage in activities and life in general. Loneliness and the never-ending thoughts of his wife and daughter's tragic death slowly and steadily wore him down. He and his son Mitchell remained estranged. Tom passed 13 years after the murders.

Then another unforeseeable incident unfolded at Jimmy and Margie's home. An early summer evening around 10:00 pm, Mitchell showed up at his sister Margie's house. Drunk and brandishing a hand gun; a 9mm semi-automatic Smith & Wesson. He knocked loudly on the Mauri's door. Jimmy opened the door and Mitchell walked in. The sight of the gun created an enormous amount of nervous tension.

Margie said, "What are you doing here? What do you want?"

Mitchell gestured toward the kitchen table and said loudly, "We need to talk, you have probably been expecting me."

Jimmy said, "We did *not* expect to hear from you or see you. Why are you here?"

Mitchell motioned again toward the kitchen table. The three of them sat in chairs around the table. Mitchell sat his gun on the right side out of reach of Jimmy and Margie.

Then he said, "I came for my share of the inheritance and insurance money."

Margie, visibly nervous and agitated said, "If you made any effort to be around when all hell rained down on our dad, you would know there is no money from his estate. He lost his dry-cleaning business, no thanks to you. He has been in a convalescent home for over two years. Did you ever one time stop in to see him? Jimmy and I helped him sell his house to pay for the medical expenses and long-term care facility. There is no money left, Mitchell. Jimmy and I have paid out-of-pocket expenses related to Dad's care. I would like to be reimbursed also, but there is no money left. And now you show up at our house *brandishing a gun* demanding something that doesn't exist? Whatever you are up to, it is not going to work."

Mitchell became quite loud and belligerent during the conversation. Margie became increasingly agitated and nervous as she too began to nearly shout at her brother.

Jimmy and Margie's son, Gary, home on leave from Fairchild Air Force Base, slept in the back bedroom. He retired to bed earlier that evening in order to catch a 6:00 A.M. flight out of LAX returning to Fairchild. The loud voices woke him up. He slipped into his BDU's (fatigues) and quietly walked down the hallway from his bedroom to locate the source of all the noise. There at the kitchen table he saw his Uncle Mitchell and his parents in a heated argument. He stood in the darkness of the hallway and could not be seen by any of the three people. Then he noticed the gun on the table. Slipping into his dad's office/work area he pulled a .357 magnum revolver out of the office desk. He loaded the .357 and slipped it into the back of his fatigues. Moving quietly down the hallway he stepped into view of his parents, Mitchell, facing Margie and Jimmy could not see his nephew. Gary lifted his finger motioning his parents not to draw attention to him.

Trained by the military in survival tactics and weaponry, Gary moved quietly, but briskly to the kitchen table. He knew a confrontation would be inevitable between himself and his estranged uncle. Gary appeared beside the table before his uncle realized that he stepped into the room. In a deliberate and quick motion, Gary picked up the 9MM from the table, ejected the magazine and cleared the chamber to assure there could not be a bullet in the gun. Mitchell did not have time to respond. Gary slid the gun into the waste line of his fatigues and put the magazine in his left pocket.

Mitchell started to rise out of his chair, but Gary placed a hand on his shoulder forcing him to remain seated. He said, "When I let you up, you are going to walk straight to the front door and out of the house. I will be right behind you."

Mitchell tried to stand up again, but Gary held him in his chair. Then he took one step backwards and allowed Mitchell to stand. The two men locked eyes. Gary stood as tall as his uncle, approximately 6 feet and 2 inches. Mitchell, now disarmed, and facing a younger man his own size and obviously in better physical condition.

Gary, without breaking eye contact said, "Front door."

Mitchell did not move.

Gary said, "Now."

Mitchell turned and started toward the front door. Gary allowed several feet between them before he followed.

Gary and his dad walked behind Mitchell until he reached his car.

Mitchell turned and said, 'Give me back my gun."

Ignoring his demand, Gary said, "Get in the car."

Mitchell hesitated. Then Jimmy said, "You made a big mistake coming over here drunk and carrying a weapon. I don't intend to call the police, but I don't know if I can talk Margie out of it. She's really pissed right now. You know that this will earn you a very lengthy prison sentence. Now, get in your car and get the hell out of here."

He opened his door and slid in behind the steering wheel. Again, he demanded to have his gun.

Gary walked around the car to the passenger side, opened the door and laid the gun on the floor of the car. Then he pulled the magazine out of his pocket and removed the seven bullets from the magazine and put the bullets in his pocket. He tossed the magazine into the back seat without taking his eyes off his uncle. He said, "You are not welcome here, ever. Don't come back."

Margie, visibly shaken, wanted to call the police. Jimmy asked her not to and said, "An arrest would certainly send him back to prison. After tonight's confrontation, it is doubtful we will ever hear from him again. If he does come back, we won't let him in and we'll call the police immediately."

Margie did not agree. She said, "What is happening? I have lost my entire family. My mom, my sister, we just buried my dad. I am so angry I could care less if my brother is alive or dead, I never want to see him again. Who knows what could have happened tonight? He could have shot all of us. Why is this happening?" Then she said in a startled voice, "Lisa, did anyone check on Lisa?"

Lisa, their youngest daughter, now a junior in high school slept in her bedroom. She planned on getting up early and going to the airport with her parents and her brother. Gary said, "I checked on her, she's sound asleep and probably won't believe any of this when we tell her about it tomorrow."

Jimmy stepped in closer to Margie and said, "Let's sleep on this and decide tomorrow if the police should be involved." Reluctantly Margie agreed.

Aftermath

Roy Warren Osborn

Osborn appealed his double murder conviction seven times. They were all denied as deemed frivolous and bearing no merit. Thirty-three years after the killings, the court commuted his sentence to two life sentences, removing the words 'without the possibility of parole.' Osborn died in prison one year later in 1998 at the age of 70. Most of that time he spent isolated from the general prison population for his own safety. He never admitted to the murders.

Mitchell—Thomas Mitchell Malloy

The only son of Tom and Inez Malloy, and brother to Norma Widick and Margie Mauri. Mitchell could not abandon the adversarial relationship that he bestowed on the people closest to him.

Mitchell slowly and steadily entered the world of drugs and pornography. He hid his lifestyle from the family that he walked away from. Trouble and failed relationships followed wherever he went. He generated an arrest record that included multiple repeat offenses. Mitchell might have found his way out, but he needed a lot of attention to pull him off of the road he chose to travel. The move across country, opening a new business, weddings, and grandkids, kept the Malloy household quite busy. Mitchell may have unintentionally become lost in the activities. Whatever the reason, he continued on a downward, non-stop spiral. Some of his secrets would not come to light until long after the horrific family tragedy. Unfortunately, one of his secrets would not be known for many more decades.

Mitchell fathered a son, born in 1962. Almost two years before the murders of his mother and sister. No one knew about his child. Inez and Norma never met their grandson and nephew. No one in the immediate family or extended family ever met his child. Mitchell moved to Florida shortly after his encounter one summer night at his sister Margie's house. It is unknown if he went to Florida for a job, or if he just wanted to get as far away from Southern California as he could. He took his then 15-year-old son and wife to Florida when he left. He continued to attract trouble from the police. The unfavorable interaction between Mitchell and law enforcement always seemed to happen when he drank alcohol or used drugs. Mitchell's son died in Florida in 1995 at the age of 33. Mitchell died in 1998 at the age of 61. He and his sister did not reconcile. He made no attempt to make amends with his father. Mitchell never revealed the existence of his son to any family member. His existence only became known through an Ancestry and Family Search conducted during the writing of this book.

Gaynard Widick

Norma's husband, born and raised in Southern California in the San Gabriel Valley.

Gaynard did not remarry after the tragic deaths of his wife and mother-in-law. He carried an enormous amount of guilt for setting the murders in motion. Gaynard could not shake his gambling addiction and drifted back and forth between Southern California and Las Vegas.

Norma's life insurance policy bore a double indemnity clause for accidental death. Gaynard received $20,000.00 from the insurance company, a lot of money in 1964. By comparison, the cost of a house in Southern California at the time of the murders: approximately $21,000.00. The price of a new car: approximately $3,000.00.

His consumption of alcohol increased as a means to escape the nightmares of the murders he believed he set in motion. Gaynard died 20 years after the murders in 1984 at the age of 47.

Norma (Malloy) Widick

Norma, the youngest daughter of Tom and Inez Malloy.

She may not have known how important and adored she became to her family and friends. Short in stature, but somehow a very large presence in the lives of everyone she knew. Tragically taken at an early age, her loss lingered amongst the family she left behind. She has always been missed. Even today, her relatives speak of her fondly and the positive impact she brought into their lives. A gifted young lady who always wanted the best for everyone.

Norma, only 22 years old, was married seven short months at the time of the murders. The victim of a series of tragic events that reached, sadly, into the hearts and minds of those that knew her and loved her.

Five years after the killings, Norma's high school photo would be enlarged again. Displayed on an easel alongside of a colorful cloth covered table. Her classmate gathered for their 10-year high school reunion. The caption below her photo read: Norma (Malloy) Widick. Gone Too Soon. Loved Everyone. Loved By Everyone.

Margie (Malloy) Mauri

Margie, the oldest sibling of Tom and Inez's children.

She carried a huge burden about the nightmare and memory of what happened to her mother and sister. She suppressed the haunting thoughts the best she could. Margie and her husband, Jimmy, poured themselves into raising their three children.

In that senseless tragic moment of the murders she lost her birth family. Her mother and sister, her best friend, were gone forever and would not see another birthday party, a holiday gathering, her kids' graduations and weddings, or other special events. She watched her father slowly die from heartbreak. She would be estranged the rest of her life from her brother, Mitchell. He chose a life style that Margie would not allow into her family, especially into the lives of her children. Her children went on and established good careers in paramedics, search and rescue, and real estate.

Margie held up a good front for a long time after the murders. The weight of the tragic killings, the loss of her father, and the conflict with her brother, eventually led to anti-depressants and other prescription drugs to help her day-to-day existence. Margie died in 1999 at the age of 67. She never spoke to Gaynard Widick after the night of the murders. She also never spoke to or heard from her brother after he came to her home drunk and carrying a weapon.

Inez Malloy

Inez (Eastwood) Malloy, the second born of seven children. Born on June 13, 1910, in Buffalo, Indiana to Henry and Carrie Eastwood. Her family moved to Fort Dodge, Iowa when she turned six years old.

Inez grew up having the opportunity to see young America survive its most difficult times. Her generation most likely saw national, and inter-national changes, unlike any other generation has ever experienced.

Inez witnessed America enter into a World War in 1917, she saw the effects of the world-wide Pandemic of 1918 (The Spanish Flu). An adventurous teenager at the height of the Roaring 20s. The Great Depression shook all of America and the world. It began on what became known as Black Thursday, October 24, 1929. Then the dust bowl hit the majority of the American Midwest. It started the year after the Great Depression in 1930, and lasted nearly 10 years. She saw the country drawn into another war, World War II. America entered the war in 1941; it ended in 1945. Sadly, she saw three United States Presidents die in office: Harding, Roosevelt and Kennedy.

Tom and Inez were married in the spring of 1932.

Their first born arrived later that year, Marjorie (Margie) Pauline Malloy. Five years later, 1937, their second born arrived, Thomas Mitchell Malloy. And, four years later, September 1941, their third child arrived, Norma Lorene Malloy. All three of their children were born in Fort Dodge, Iowa.

Almost nineteen years after their wedding, Tom and Inez moved their family to Alhambra, California. Southern California would be everything Inez imagined it to be, wonderful, sub-tropical weather, beautiful coastlines, and splendid mountainous areas. They lived in the San Gabriel Valley, an area rich in agriculture. Inez often spoke of her happiness and life she and her family enjoyed. Two of her brothers, Chuck and Louis, and two of her sisters, Vera and Helen, and their families, followed Inez to Southern California. One sister, Dorothy, and her husband Lloyd Ponsness, moved to Rathdrum, Idaho. Her oldest brother, William (Buster), remained in Fort Dodge.

Inez just began another chapter in her life, three grandchildren became the brightest part of her good life. She was 53 years old.

Tom Malloy

Born and raised in the Midwest: Fort Dodge, Iowa, his parents owned and operated a dry-cleaning business. He always liked the sport of boxing. Tom could often be found pursuing a caveat of prize money from one of the local taverns hosting boxing matches.

Some well-known actors, before they were well known, attempted to enter the boxing sport, trying to make a career out of the event. One of those pre-actor boxers was Buddy Ebsen of the 'Jed Clampett, Beverly Hillbillies' fame. Before Buddy Ebsen entered acting, he would tour around parts of the country on a boxing circuit. One of his stops: Fort Dodge, Iowa. Tom signed up for an exhibition boxing match against Buddy Ebsen. He frequently talked about that event expressing a fond memory. Tom, soundly defeated by the more experienced boxer/turned actor, always talked about it as an unforgettable, memorable experience.

Just after the end of WWII, Tom became involved in another boxing event. It happened the night he knocked out the local champ in a fight that brought him $50.00. One of the local taverns offered prize money for lasting a specified number of rounds in the ring opposing the local favorite. This event perpetuated Tom's reputation as a formidable opponent in the ring. He did not do much boxing after that. Family life and working at the family business took most of his available time. His boxing hobby did not rise up on the priority list any longer.

After the tragedy of the murders, Tom slowly and steadily lost his health and his will to carry on. In less than a year after the killings, he closed his dry-cleaning business. He found it increasingly difficult to continue the business that he and his wife started.

One Saturday afternoon, he fell asleep in a rocking chair while watching tv. Smoking a cigarette when he fell asleep, and the arm of the chair caught on fire. Tom survived the mishap but this only caused more concern about his ability to be alone.

The horrific details of the murders and those final moments of his wife and daughter prevented him from getting peace and closure. He often reflected on the 'what-ifs': what if I made that trip with my wife and daughter to Las Vegas; what if that damn key did not break; what if Gaynard did not disappear? He could not get that fateful night out of his mind, and the horror his wife and daughter experienced.

The big, strong, man had been brought to his knees by one of life's unforeseeable sucker punches. Tom never found the will to get back up. It left him sad, heartbroken, and lonely. He did not attempt to speak to the accused and determine for himself the killer's guilt or innocence. The jury decided that for him.

He did not have the energy to chase down his son and work on that relationship. Realizing that Mitchell did not want to return home and rejoin the family, Tom let him have his way. His paranoia that someone was watching him, eased a bit when his niece and her family rented his home, and he moved into the detached garage/apartment. Two years after the murders his niece moved her family out of the area, and his house rented to people he did not know. Tom remained in the detached garage/apartment on the same property. His brother-in-law, Chuck, stopped by to check on Tom as often as time would allow. Then he, too, moved his family to Idaho two years after the killings.

Tom was admitted to a nursing home in the mid 1970s. He died there in 1977, thirteen years after the loss of his wife and daughter. Tom Malloy never knew his grandson, Mitchell's son, born two years before the murders. The boy carried his name and died a few years before Tom.

Acknowledgements

I want to start by thanking my cousin, Gary Mauri, the grandson and nephew of the victims. We conferred often as I gathered information on these homicides. I also want to thank my cousin, Toni Eastwood. She is a critical writing instructor in California. Toni convinced me to change the book from a narrative to a dialogue form; I am glad she did. Thanks to my cousin Marty Erickson, a retired judge in Iowa. She led me through the complicated legal aspects of an arrest and trial.

Family Search revealed unexpected findings on one family member, the victims' son and brother, Thomas Mitchell Malloy, that is highlighted in the epilogue.

Special thanks to the (Las Vegas) Clark County Library District. They allowed me to go through their archives on all the newspaper articles written about the murders. Thanks to the reporters that doggedly covered the story from beginning to end. Thanks to the Las Vegas Metropolitan Police Department. They helped me identify the location of the crime, and the changes that occurred in the city since the time of the killings. They also informed me that the accused died in prison.

Special thanks to my sister, Sandy Marion, and my daughters; Alicia and Valerie. They read the story multiple times, and gave feedback on the many additions, and situations that occurred in the book. Thank you to my long-time friend, Fred Fricke, who researched and helped identify the factual accuracy of the era.

Thank you also, to the many, many people that discussed the losses they have dealt with in their lives. One of those stories involved the wife of my childhood friend, George Cooper. His wife Vannareth became a victim of the Khmer Rouge in Cambodia. Fleeing the tyranny, she and her family were captured. She witnessed the execution of her three brothers and was forcibly separated from her mother and grandmother, imprisoned in a labor camp for nearly four years. Eventually she made it to America where she met George, completed nursing school and they started a family of their own. The once frequent nightmares have slowed, but are not gone.

A common thread amongst those that experienced the loss of loved ones, expected and unexpected, is that closure is difficult. In some cases, there is no closure. Family and friends become all too important at a time of loss.

And finally, a belated thanks to my dad, Chuck Eastwood. He reminded us and reminded us, until it became second nature to check the back seat. Friends and relatives on their journey to learning how to drive would not escape his schooling.

I also want to recognize the support groups, crisis counselors, and members of the clergy that unselfishly come alongside of people suffering tragic losses. They provide the much-needed hope during a most devastating time. Tragedy and the loss of loved ones almost always happens unexpectedly, it is always devastating. Navigating through the loss can be a very different journey for some than it is for others.

A time for grieving is important; forgetting is impossible. Many people can relate to the victims' husband and father in this true crime book. Tom Malloy never found closure.

About the Author

Photo Source: Dee Eastwood

Doug Eastwood loves the outdoors. He moved his family to North Idaho in 1978 and has enjoyed every day in the Idaho Panhandle. Married for 48 years, he has two daughters and two granddaughters. Once an avid bicyclist, he recorded tens of thousands of miles pedaling all over the Pacific Northwest and parts of Canada. He enjoys cross-country skiing, snow-shoeing, ATV and UTV riding, and woodworking. He played softball for decades and actively enjoys the high participatory sport of bowling.

He spent over 40 years in the profession of Parks and Recreation. Most of that time, he served as the Parks Director for the City of Coeur d'Alene, Idaho. He continues to be involved with foundations and boards that promote public outdoor recreation, including serving six years on the State of Idaho Parks and Recreation Board. He also participated in a local service club, Kiwanis, for nearly 30 years. On March 17th, 2023 he had the honor and privilege of being the Grand Marshall in the Coeur d'Alene St. Patrick's Day Parade.

His first book, *The North Idaho Centennial Trail—The Trail that Almost Wasn't,* is a historical non-fiction documentary about an iconic multi-use trail system in the area where he currently resides.

Printed in the USA
CPSIA information can be obtained
at www.ICGtesting.com
LVHW042017310124
770343LV00002B/11